D0947315

THE

CHALLENGE
FROM THE EAST

AND THE

REBIRTH OF THE WEST

The
Challenge
from the East

and the

Rebirth of the West

Michael Spicer

ST. MARTIN'S PRESS/NEW YORK

A THOMAS DUNNE BOOK.

An imprint of St. Martin's Press.

Design by Julie Duquet

Library of Congress Cataloging-in-Publication Data

Spicer, Michael.
    The Challenge from the East and the rebirth of the West /
by Michael Spicer.—1st ed.
        p.   cm.
    "A Thomas Dunne book."
    ISBN 0-312-14293-5
    1. International trade. 2. International economic
relations. 3. Balance of power. 4. International
relations.   I. Title.
HF1379.S694   1996
382—dc20   96-6939
                                            CIP

First Edition: June 1996

10   9   8   7   6   5   4   3   2   1

The tendency of human beings, and of statesmen—who are human beings—is . . . to think that their own wretched lives are confined to some sixty or seventy years, therefore it is open to them to force an anticipation of the results which the national play of forces and of affections and the alteration of the judgements and the mutual feelings of various peoples in the world will bring before us.

—Lord Salisbury, May 7, 1902, when prime minister of Britain

CONTENTS

ACKNOWLEDGMENTS

I AM DEEPLY grateful to Daniel Hannan for all his help both in the research and drafting of this book.

MY SINCEREST THANKS go also to the Olin Foundation of New York for their generous sponsorship of the project, and to the American Enterprise Institute, the Manhattan Institute, and the Heritage Foundation for their assurances of support in its promotion. As has been the case with each of the seven books I have written, Margaret Bottomley has done the typing and corrected mistakes in the writing. Thank you, Margaret.

I ALSO WANT to thank my friend Malcolm Wallop, former Senator for Wyoming, who with the assistance of Jack Copeland and through the medium of the Big Horn Mountain Foundation has done so much to inspire the direction of this book.

THANK YOU ALSO to Tom Dunne, one of New York's greatest publishers, for his continued faith in my writings and for sticking to his arguments against much of their content; on several occasions it has greatly clarified my own thinking.

LASTLY, MY WIFE, Ann, has as ever put up with my scratching late into the night in my office at the top of our house in Cropthorne. I promise her that now that this has been completed, and before I begin work on my next book, I will at least tidy away (not necessarily the same as throw away) the mass of old newspapers that litter every corner of the room.

I DEDICATE THIS book to my Alma Mater, the British Conservative Party, currently in the doldrums; if it sticks to the nostrums of Free Trade it will not long remain there.

Michael Spicer
Cropthorne, 1996

THE CHALLENGE FROM THE EAST AND THE REBIRTH OF THE WEST

THE EASTERN ECONOMIC Miracle is now a fact of history. For the past decade the major countries of the Orient, representing half the world's population, have been growing at phenomenal rates, in some cases up to five times the pace of their counterparts in the West. The point is made graphically in Figs. 1 and 2. Whereas most Western countries consider themselves lucky if they achieve an annual rate of economic growth of 3 percent—especially if they sustain this over a period of years—China, for example, has in recent years consistently notched up rates of over 10 percent. Given the absolute size of China, humankind has never before witnessed such a massive transformation.

THE CRUDE STATISTICS are mind boggling. According to the International Energy Agency in Paris, China will require one new large electricity power station every week for the next 15 years, giving her 280 gigawatts of new capacity between 1996 and 2010. In that year she will be importing 3 million barrels of oil a day—more than the entire output of the North Sea at its

Fig. 1

GROWTH OF REAL GDP
Percent per annum

Period	USA	Japan	EU	4 NIAE(a)	PR China
1987	3.1%	4.1%	2.9%	11.9%	10.9%
1988	3.9	6.2	4.2	9.5	11.3
1989	2.5	4.7	3.4	6.3	4.3
1990	1.2	4.8	3.0	7.1	3.8
1991	−0.6	4.3	1.1	7.8	8.2
1992	2.3	1.1	1.0	5.7	13.1
1993	3.1	−0.2	−0.4	6.0	13.7
1994	4.1	0.6	2.8	7.2	12.0
1995 (b)	3.2	1.8	3.2	6.8	n.a.
1996 (b)	1.9	3.5	3.1	6.6	n.a.
Averages: 1977−86	2.7	4.0	2.1	8.1	9.0
1987−96	2.5	3.1	2.4	7.5	9.6 (c)

(a) Four newly industrialised Asian economies; Hong Kong, Singapore, Korea, and Taiwan.

(b) Forecast.

(c) Average for 1987 to 1994.

Source: IMF "World Economic Outlook," May 1995.

peak. She will also be emitting more carbon dioxide into the atmosphere than all the 32 nations of the OECD put together.

As pointed out in the World Bank's "Global Economic Prospects," published in 1995 if all goes on in the same way, by the year 2020 China will have overtaken the United States as the largest economic power on earth. Britain will rank in the mid-teens, below Taiwan, Thailand, Indonesia, and South Korea. This means that if present trends prevail the West will lose its economic pre-eminence to the East. It is a fair assumption that there will be a new balance, perhaps a reversal, in the relative military positions of the East and the West.

What is far less clear is whether the implications of all this have been properly assessed in the West. Reactions there are mixed, not to say muddled. Some people are mesmerized by it, caught like the proverbial deer in the headlights of an oncoming car. Others shrug it off as being distant and irrelevant until the competitive effect of imports hits their jobs. Then they shout at their politicians to do something about it, by which they mean put a stop to what they define as "unfair" trade. Some of the more imaginative of them simply panic. They see the whole process as the undoing of Western hegemony, to which the right response for the West is to abandon much of its culture, its belief in individual rights, and its sense of identity, and to cower behind protectionist walls.

With the ending of the Cold War, it all looked so very different at first. The triumph of capitalism and democracy over Soviet Communism was initially interpreted as the climactic confirmation of the supremacy of Western values.

This was, however, based on a misinterpretation of the nature of the Cold War. Contrary to most opinion at the time, the struggle between Soviet Communism and Western capitalism was virtually irrelevant to the long-term relationship between the Occident and the Orient. The idea, first mooted by Francis Fukuyama,* that, because the Cold War was over there was now an end to ideology, was particularly misleading. Quite to the contrary, the end of hostility between the United States and the Soviet Union and their respective allies itself paved the way for a wider—possibly more dangerous—competition between the West and the real East: rivalry between old and deep-rooted politico-religious philosophies, something that the struggle between Soviet Communism and capitalism never was. Christian humanism and

---

*"The End of History?" *The National Interest* 16 (1989).

Fig. 2

GROWTH OF REAL GDP
Percent per annum

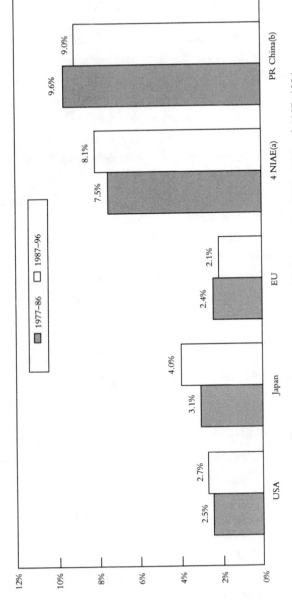

(a) Hong-Kong, Singapore, Korea, and Taiwan, (b) Averages for 1977–1986 and 1987–1994.
Source: IMF "World Economic Outlook," May 1995.

Confucian paternalism are powerful adversaries, not only as philosophies of government but as the basis for economic development.

There can be no doubting the growing tension and mistrust between East and West. What is surprising is that this should be accompanied by something of a reversal in their respective long-established outlooks, the West—quite against the grain of history—being increasingly concerned to protect and to centralize and the East to engage in commercial adventure.

It is important to be clear what is at stake. The world could no doubt ride out a shift in the relative positions of power of the East and the West. It is sad for the once all-powerful countries of the West to find themselves overtaken in terms of economic prowess by erstwhile "developing" countries, but this may not itself be calamitous in terms of the wider stability of the world.

What *is* potentially catastrophic, and what has provided me with the reason for writing this book, is the prospect of an increasingly confident but still resentful East and an inward-looking, defensive West confronting each other. Whether this is done consciously or by default does not matter. That way lies confronting the risk of war of a devastating kind.

If the stability of the world is to be assured, it must be through the spread of free trade. In the process, not only will greater wealth be created, it will be more evenly spread around, as nations become more closely interlocked. The forms of government that will arise in consequence will not be identical (in many respects they will remain antithetical), but there will be sufficient commonality among them for any threat of war based purely on suspicion of one another's political and economic systems to recede. Greater economic wealth leads ultimately to the introduction of some form of democracy, and thus of the growing confidence of formerly tyrannical regimes in their own legitimacy. Such countries tend to lose any latent expansionist claims and begin to live at peace with their neighbors.

What is more, it is clearly the case that the West will retain sufficient leverage for a few more years to press the pace of political reform even within the most powerful of the Confucian states. The question is whether her leading members have the will to use that leverage.

It is a matter of supreme irony and a great worry from the point of view of world stability that, at this moment of all times, the West should have begun to lose faith in the values associated with free trade and upon which over hundreds of years it has constructed its mighty economic prowess. The question, which I shall not attempt to answer until the end, is whether anything can be done to reverse this situation; on the response to this hangs very largely the issue of what is to be the state of relations between East and West throughout the twenty-first century. It matters enormously whether or not the West reestablishes its belief in free trade. If East and West are not to trade freely with each other, then, inevitably, the world is in for a rough passage; there are too many differences and rivalries between the Occident and the Orient for this not to be so. What makes the whole matter of more than passing significance is that the leading countries in each area will in the next century be armed to the teeth with strategic nuclear weapons.

CHAPTER ONE

THE RISE AND RISE AND THE LOSS OF NERVE OF THE WEST

THE STATE OF the world at the end of the twentieth century constitutes a paradox. By any measure of temporal power—economic, cultural, military—the West, in particular its leading member, the United States, reigns supreme. Its most recent triumph was clear-cut: Soviet Communism lies in tatters.

Western countries are not only richer many times over than countries in most other parts of the globe; they have a command over technology, especially military technology, that astounds even the most sophisticated of their own citizens. One calls to mind the terms of wonderment used in 1991 by Western journalists in Baghdad to describe the passage of missiles fired from American ships hundreds of miles away as they passed by hotel windows, turned street corners, entered doors, and exploded their military targets.

With the exception of Tokyo, which I will be discussing in more detail later, the capital cities that dominate the finances and the governance of the world are Washington, Berlin, London, Paris, Brussels, Rome, Geneva, The Hague, and, increasingly, Madrid.

Moscow and Beijing are important more for what they might do in the future than for any preeminence they hold at present.

Western ambassadors take the lead in all the great councils of the world—the United Nations, the World Bank, and the IMF. One of the reasons for this is that Western countries foot most of their bills. Western supremacy is not absolute, nor does its writ run unchallenged; many citizens in Bosnia must wish that it did. But if the West acts in concert, as was virtually the case in the face of Iraqi aggression in Kuwait in 1990–91, there is very little that can gainsay it.

In this sense, we live in a period of *pax occidentale*. And yet, ironically, paradoxically, extraordinarily, and possibly tragically, all is not well in the West.

In his book *The Waning of the Middle Ages*, Jan Huizinga wrote: "At the close of the Middle Ages, a sombre melancholy weighs on people's souls."

So it is today with the West. Just as one would have expected the age of the Renaissance to have ushered in a period of great optimism, so today in the West one would have expected the flowering of self-confidence, a savoring of the knowledge that its ethics and ethos, developed over thousands of years, to have finally triumphed.

But that is not how it is. On the contrary, in place of self-confidence, there is self-doubt. It is worse than that: in place of a sense of security, there is a growing fear. It is directed in a general fashion toward what is loosely called the East and, in particular, toward mainland China.

The recent origin of this new angst lies in the recognition of the emergence of a massive economic challenge to the West. The idea is growing that the combination of cheap labor in the East and ready access there to the latest technology and to capital will, if nothing changes, be the economic undoing of Europe and of North America. Quite simply, it is said, the industries of the West will be overpowered. The feat of unmatchable economic rivalry, when combined with growing military strength, especially of China, is seen to threaten the very foundations of the Western democratic political structure.

As with the reaction to most bogies, the fear has some genuine foundation. Napoleon may not have had an air force of hot air balloons at his disposal, nor the wherewithal to build a Channel tunnel, but he did have a large army and a large navy targeted at invading England. As at the turn of the eighteenth century, so at the end of this one. The combination of myth and fact may lead to fanciful and irrational conclusions. These in turn may lead to action by which the worst fears are fulfilled.

It is now commonplace to acknowledge that within the next few years China, if she holds together as a single state, will overtake the United States as the world's largest economy; nor can there be much dispute that she and other states in the region will become major nuclear powers; nor that Confucianism has led and will continue to lead to a very different form of government in China from that of states where political ethos is based on the Judeo-Christian tradition.

But to argue from this that the game is up for the West, that the time has come for it to abandon beliefs—especially about free trade and enterprise—developed and tested over thousands of years, is manifestly overreactive. And yet, fanned on each side of the Atlantic by such populist politicians as Pat Buchanan and James Goldsmith, that is precisely what is happening. The view is undoubtedly gaining ground that the only hope now for the West is to retreat into the shell of protected, centrally managed, and mutually exclusive trade blocs. With this goes the belief that it has become unrealistic to press for a world order based on Western-nurtured concepts of human liberty. It is not even clear, when one considers, for instance, the nature of some of the institutions emerging at the center of the most advanced trade bloc, the European Union, that in the devising of political structures, any particular priority continues to be attached in the West to democratic values.

The enormity of this situation is fully apparent only when one considers how well founded and how coherent and, indeed, how triumphant Western values—especially those related to the freedom of trade—have been thought to be. Their pedigree is certainly a long one. Their roots are deep and traceably so. Their essence is capable of careful definition. Simply stated, it is that humankind can, through the application of reason, further its own interests and seek greater fulfilment. It is possible that, in pursuit of their own needs, people may damage those of others around them. To resolve clashes of interest and prevent a general slide into anarchy, common rules and methods of adjudication must be established and enforced. The government (executive, legislative, and judiciary aspects) required for this purpose should, however, be carefully circumscribed to prevent it from overstepping this limited role.

Over the last two hundred years, the view emerged that the best way to control a government was to require it to be dissolved at regular intervals and reforged according to popular wishes. The primary function of democratic government was thus to maximize the well-being of the people as defined and judged by the people themselves. Checks had to be built into the system to guard against a "dictatorship" of the majority; principally these were to take the form of guaranteed rights enforced by independent magistrates.

The different ideological strands of Western politics—conservatism, socialism, liberalism—all had this central core of beliefs. Their various exponents argued their different points using the same idiom and accepting common rules. John Locke's skeptical view of the role and legitimacy of the state differed radically from that of Thomas Hobbes, but they each stood shoulder to shoulder against, for instance, the Islamic, Buddhist, and Confucian traditions, in which individual rights are simply not a meaningful concept.

The ground rules of modern Western political thought were largely drawn up by the thinkers of eighteenth-century Europe—David Hume in Scotland, Charles Montesquieu and Claude Helvétius in France, Cesare Beccaria in Italy, and Benjamin Franklin in North America. The political principles that most captured the spirit of the Age of Reason and defined subsequent Western politics were those encompassed by the United States Constitution, the Declaration of Independence, and the other statements that emerged from the American Revolution.*

Nor should philosophical development in the rest of the Americas be forgotten: Simón Bolívar and José de San Martín are classic products of the Age of Reason who would have been instantly recognized by Jefferson or Voltaire as kindred spirits: educated, progressive, Masonic, rational. The constitutions for which they fought were based around the concept of limited government and inalienable human rights.

A key feature of the Western tradition is the doctrine of liberal nationalism. All discussions of the role of the state and the place of the individual within it demand these questions: *How is the state to be defined? Where should the boundaries be drawn of the entity within which these issues are to be addressed?*

In the West, the answer that emerged from the period of Enlightenment is that a state should include only those who sense that

---

*Max, Beloff, ed. *The Debate on the American Revolution 1761–1785*, (New York, 1989).

they have sufficient common identity to feel able to accept government from one another—that is to say, a nation. A sense of community can derive from many things: a common language, a unifying religion, or a shared history. But ultimately, under Western principles, it must be for people themselves to define their own nationhood. Once they have done so, their right to statehood should be respected. This is a far cry from considerations of geography, history, administrative convenience, or the state of diplomatic relations with neighboring states.

It is the rational, tolerant nationalism of Jean-Jacques Rousseau and Johann Herder, of George Canning and Frantisek Palacký. Perhaps its most prolific champion was the nineteenth-century Italian patriot Giuseppe Mazzini, who laid down the doctrine that every distinct people should form an independent, unitary, and self-governing political unit. Working closely with liberals from across Europe, including Louis Kossuth and Alexandre Ledru-Rollin, he based his demands for democracy on the slogan "Where there is a nation, let there be a state." Liberal democracy, reasoned eighteenth- and nineteenth-century political philosophers, could not function without the willingness of the citizen to accept certain obligations as well as rights. When the legitimacy of the state was challenged by a cohesive group, democracy was put under severe strain. Better, then, for those who are disaffected to administer their own affairs than for the state to exist within artificial boundaries and by suppressive means.

The ideal of nationality was crucial to the rise of liberalism across the world. Liberal nationalists have a distinguished history of resistance to authoritarianism, be it against the reactionary oligarchy upheld by Clemens Metternich and the post-1815 governments of Europe, the racially based dictatorship of the Nazis, or the tyranny of the Soviet police state.

In the West the concept of democratic self-determination has been linked with that of personal freedom.

From a disciple of Jeremy Bentham came a definition of individual liberty that has yet to be supplanted in Western politics. "The only freedom which deserves the name, is that of pursuing our own good in our own way so long as we do not attempt to deprive others of theirs, or impede their efforts to obtain it," wrote J. S. Mill in his essay "On Liberty." As with Bentham's definition of utility, Mill's description of liberty has become a centerpiece of Western politics. All Western democratic politicians have nominally devoted themselves to the ends of personal freedom and general happiness, whether or not they consciously see themselves as liberals or utilitarians.

While Bentham and Mill may have produced some of the most distilled and thorough statements of the rational-liberal Western creed, they represent no more than the culmination of the ideas that over time have set the Western tradition apart.

Aristotle and Plato set in motion a train of philosophical thought that was to run through the ages to Philip Sidney and Francis Bacon in the sixteenth century, to John Locke and Isaac Newton in the seventeenth, to James Madison and Jean-Jacques Rousseau in the eighteenth, to Richard Cobden and Camillo di Cavour in the nineteenth. From its earliest roots, with very few deviations, Western philosophy has held to a view of man as being self-motivated and rational.

It is a matter of some importance to be clear how uniquely "Western" is this view. Confucian political philosophy is, by contrast, essentially concerned with how the government should administer its subjects. The law is seen not as a guarantor of individual rights or of justice but as a means of preserving order. In the Muslim world there is no corpus of secular thought comparable to that in the West; the vast majority of political and economic ideology is based around the need to structure society according to God's laws. In the greater part of Africa, the concept of enforceable individual rights existed only during the period of colonial administration.

Western liberalism has roots that stretch deep into the Judeo-Christian tradition. The essence of the imagery of the Garden of Eden is that man, having defied God by tasting the forbidden fruit, became aware of right and wrong. Man was possessed of free will, able to choose good or evil. This perspective is entirely lacking from the Islamic version of the story. From its earliest days, the Judeo-Christian tradition has emphasized personal responsibility: the ability of man consciously to choose to do good. By contrast, in the Islamic tradition the notion of man's free will is almost nonexistent (the word *Muslim* means "surrendered man"). It is almost wholly absent also from the philosophies of the Far East. Confucian, Taoist, and Buddhist teachings (as well as the Japanese offshoot, Shinto) all stress the virtues of obedience, stoicism, contemplation, acceptance of one's lot. At the heart of Confucianism lies the belief that earthly existence is out of harmony with the Way of Heaven. The prime duty of man is to strive, through the medium of complex rituals and reverence, for ancestors to bring life on earth into step with the government of the universe. Government exists as an intermediary between man and the gods. Obedience to authority is therefore of supreme importance. To the Taoist, the key virtue is passivity. Action for its own sake will put man at odds with the natural order around him. It is far better to accept and enjoy one's place than to strive to change it. For the Buddhist, the aim of life is to transcend the pains and illusions of the "world of dust" and, through tranquility and contemplation, to reach a state of nirvana ("no wind").

The importance of free will is unique to the Judeo-Christian tradition transmitted by theologians such as St. Augustine and John Duns Scotus. What count are an individual's thoughts and actions, not his contribution to a successful group or his cheerful acceptance of authority.

John Milton provides perhaps the most eloquent statement of the place of rational free will in Christianity. Milton was obsessed by the theme of liberty. To him, liberty was both a political doctrine and a moral state. It was not ensured through the abolition of rules (this Milton called license and heartily disliked); rather, it was derived from a sense of inner freedom, of moral purity. Writing during the turbulent years of the mid-seventeenth century, he saw the political struggle between liberty and slavery as mirroring an inner struggle between virtue and vice. Charles I became a tyrant because he allowed his appetites to rule him; Cromwell defeated the tyranny by overcoming his own vice. In *Paradise Lost*, Milton illustrates the central importance of the Fall to Christian theology. Man *chose*, God's omnipotence notwithstanding, to eat the forbidden fruit: "They themselves decreed their own revolt, not I," says Milton's God. From that action, man's capacity for free will has remained his chief religious attribute. Man has a duty to use his reason freely to turn to God. God, for His part, will stand up to open-minded rational investigation from man.

"Herein He appears to us as it were in human shape, enters into a covenant with us, swears to keep it, binds Himself like a just lawgiver to His own prescriptions, gives Himself to be understood by men, judges and is judged, measures and is commensurate to right reason." (From "The Doctrine and Discipline of Divorce Restored to the Good of Both Sexes.")

Here is a ringing assertion of the rational-liberal element in the Judeo-Christian tradition. The individual's duty is not to obey unthinkingly but to use reason freely to inquire into God's legal justice. Good can derive only from a free application of logic: "Opinion in good men is but knowledge in the making" ("Areopatgitica"). Popes and priests, Milton concludes, should be prevented from denying the capacity for reason to the masses. If people do not choose virtue of their own free will and accord, theirs is not true virtue.

The Reformation produced the breed of Christianity that placed the strongest emphasis on individualism, but Luther was drawing on the entire breadth of the Christian tradition. Just as the utilitarian-liberal doctrine is an especially pure form of what distinguishes Western political thought, so Protestantism is a distillation of what distinguishes Western theology. The binding of the two has given to Western culture its special force.

In its entire history, the West has produced only one lasting ideology that denies the liberal-rational view of man: Marxism. To be sure, Marxists tried to cloud the waters with talk of positive freedoms and false consciousness. What cannot be denied is that communism directly contradicts the individual's right freely to further his own happiness. Marxism is the exception that proves the rule.

Precisely for this reason, Marxism never caught on in Western industrial nations like Britain and Germany, as Marx himself had intended. Finding nowhere to take root in the West, it grew only in the authoritarian soil of Russia and China, where the traditions of hierarchy and obedience were well established and notions of individual liberty barely understood.

Capitalism has emerged out of more than two thousand years of Western civilization. It is the ultimate economic expression of that civilization: millions of individuals making rational economic decisions in their own interests and therefore in the economic interests of the wider society. Free trade and a free economy are as integral a part of the European-American tradition as democracy, human rights, and the rule of law. Capitalism could not have evolved elsewhere, nor could Western culture have developed without it.

There is, indeed, an empirical link between the West's rationalist, liberal philosophies and its record as the world's primary source of technological progress. It has been said that Europe could not have invented Einstein without having first produced Aristotle. Veneration for *"l'uomo universale"*—the all-around individual genius—was not merely a characteristic of the Renaissance period. It is part and parcel of the Western psyche. Western figures have, like Aristotle, combined an interest in politics and philosophy with a passion for scientific discovery. Of the thinkers most closely associated with the development of the Western rationalist tradition, several were also the most distinguished scientists of their day, Sir Isaac Newton, Joseph Priestley, and Benjamin Franklin being the supreme examples. A glance at a list of the Fellows of the Royal Society in the seventeenth or eighteenth century reveals an extraordinary set of overlapping interests: physics, politics, alchemy, astronomy, theology, architecture, jurisprudence, biology, and metaphysics. Our modern political system is largely the creation of empirical, scientific minds, and those minds were themselves the products of a rational-individualist culture.

To an alien looking down on the world five hundred years ago, Europe and North America would have seemed unlikely prospects for ultimate world hegemony. The great civilizations of the East would have appeared on the surface to be far more advanced, with wonderful libraries and temples, disciplined armies and navies. The Muslim world possessed great universities staffed with accomplished mathematicians, cartographers, and surgeons; India was filled with extraordinary architectural marvels; China possessed a vast population, great cities, canals, printing presses, and paper money. According to Audrea Boltho's 1994 World Bank paper, in 1500 China had the highest per capita income in the world. Here was indeed the largest economy until it was overtaken by Britain's in the 1830s. And yet, over a period of several hundreds of years, at least until the fourth quarter of the twentieth century, the West raced ahead of the East.

Why was it that the scattered peoples at the western tip of the Eurasian landmass pulled so far ahead of all the other civilizations and subsequently transmitted their success across the Atlantic?

It is a question of some importance. Rooted in its philosophical traditions, the West developed polities, institutions, and commercial practices suited to sustained economic development. The Australian historian E. L. Jones, in a seminal study, argues that the key to Europe's success was that while the other civilizations became centralized as empires (Ottoman, Mogul, and Ming), Europe remained a diverse plurality of competing states. While the Oriental empires became heavily taxed, regulated, bureaucratized, and introverted, Europe remained varied, disunited, and adventurous. Above all, the countries that made up Europe and, subsequently, the Americas, were free to trade.

Europe's nations were forced into a frantic competition with one another. The diversity of approaches and conditions meant that each country vied to emulate and improve on the best features of its neighbors—whether in terms of organization, technology, or political doctrine.

There developed a clear and unique attitude to international commerce, which the West's philosophical and religious tradition both created and nurtured. By contrast, China forbade the construction of seagoing ships in 1436, at the very time when Henry the

Navigator was planning his expeditions. Competition acted as a constant spur to the West's success: competition between individuals, between nations, between religions, between ideologies. No European state could afford the complacent isolationism of the Oriental empires.

As a result, from the sixteenth century onward, the dominance of the people of Europe became ever more evident. For more than four centuries, the West's hegemony rested in part on its technological supremacy but also on the global adventurousness of its peoples—both of which in turn stemmed from its unique approach to religion, politics, and economics. There has been, in other words, a clear line moving from the religious and moral values to the political and economic. The roots of free trade and enterprise go very deep.

It is unimaginable that at any point in the past five hundred years any European or North American monarch or political leader would have uttered words remotely similar to those delivered in 1793 by the Manchu emperor, Quaniong, to the British emissary, Lord Macartney: "There is nothing we lack nor do we need any of your country's manufactures." It is, however, entirely possible that precisely the same words could have been spoken by Chairman Mao.

The irony is that at the moment when Mao's successor, Deng Xiaoping, began to open China to some of the rigors of free trade, to the apparently great advantage of that country, signs emerged of a severe weakening of faith in the West in the political and economic principles that had served it so well and for so long.

CHAPTER TWO

THE TRADE BLOCKERS

THE CLEAREST INDICATION that there has been a faltering of Western self-confidence is in the new attitudes emerging there on the crucial issue of the freedom of trade. The movement of opinion toward greater protectionism was at first a subtle one that had its origins well before the perceived emergence of a threat from the East. Its philosophical roots in the West lay primarily in post–World War II Europe, and it was directed at first largely against the United States.

It has rarely taken the form of a crude frontal attack on the simple notion of trade itself. Even today there is little argument in the West about the merits of what is termed "fair" trade. The notion of "fairness" in trade is usually defined in terms of "level playing fields" which when carried to a logical conclusion is a contradiction in terms. Trade, after all, largely exists to satisfy the needs of *different* economies. If all the differences are wiped out, there is not much point in trading.

One of the reasons for the continued reluctance in the West to abandon support for the notion of free trade is that since World

War II at least, trade expansion has by and large gone hand in hand with a rise in living standards. Cause-and-effect is debatable, but the historical facts are that from 1953 to 1963, world trade grew at 6.1 percent and world income grew at 4.3 percent; between 1963 and 1973 the figures were 8.9 percent and 5.1 percent respectively. As it happens, these two periods together almost exactly match the great days of tariff reductions, beginning with the GATT Geneva Round in 1947. During the first thirty years of GATT (General Agreement on Tariffs and Trade), the United States alone reduced her tariffs by an average of 92 percent. The authority on post-World War II trade patterns, Professor Jagdish Bhagwati of the Massachusetts Institute of Technology, has written, "If tariff cuts lead to more trade and more trade produces more income and more income facilitates more tariff cuts, the result is a "virtuous circle" that can produce the level of prosperity we saw in the glorious 1950s and 1960s." (*Protectionism*; MIT Press, 1988.)

By the mid-1970s, however, a subtle change was occurring in the trade policies of most Western countries. Despite the completion of the Tokyo Round of GATT in 1979, followed most recently by the Uruguay Round, tariff reductions began to be accompanied by Western governments' erection of a growing number of nontariff barriers—most notably a plethora of so-called voluntary export restraints and antidumping measures where the artficially low price of a good is used as a reason for restraining its import. In the last twenty years these have largely wiped out the "virtuous" effect of the tariff reductions. Growth rates of both world output and trade have been correspondingly noticeably slower in the last twenty years than they were in the previous twenty, as is shown when the figures for growth rates in the 1960s quoted above are compared with those in Fig. 3 below.

In the face of these statistics, the argument has arisen that while

Fig. 3

AVERAGE ANNUAL GROWTH RATES: GDP AND EXPORTS

	GDP growth		Export growth	
	1970–80	1980–93	1970–80	1980–93
India	3.4%	5.2%	5.9%	7.0%
South Korea	10.1	9.1	22.7	12.3
Singapore	8.3	6.9	4.2	12.7
Taiwan	n.a.	n.a.	16.5	10.0
Hong Kong	9.2	6.5	9.9	15.8
World	3.6	2.9	4.0	n.a.

Source: *World Development Report, IMF, 1995.*

a liberal trade policy may be good for the prosperity of the world as a whole, individual countries who open up their markets to foreign competition may suffer, either because their industries are ravaged by those of other countries or because they are subject to the "unfairness" of "uneven playing fields."

Widely held such a view may be, but the empirical evidence for it is weak. The argument for protection should be at its strongest with respect to developing countries. They, after all, have weak home markets, lack the foreign exchange to purchase advanced technology, and are subject to bullying from powerful foreigners. The evidence, even in the case of "weak" developing countries, is overwhelmingly against protectionism. Compare, for instance, the economic fortunes of a sample of nonoil-producing developing countries east of the Suez Canal. Take India, whose academic and political fraternities have until recently been among the most articulate exponents over the past forty years of the notion of protected and balanced growth within the supposed confines of scarce foreign capital. As shown in Fig. 3, protectionist India's growth has been at a considerably slower pace than those of the relatively open economies of South Korea, Taiwan, Singapore, and Hong Kong. Here again is Professor Bhagwati in *Protectionism*:

> *Take the compelling contrast between South Korea and India— prime examples of trade-liberalizing and protectionist regimes. South Korea's manufacturing exports, negligible in 1962, amounted by 1980 to nearly four times those of India. South Korea's manufacturing sector was less than 25 percent as large as India's in 1970 (measured in terms of value added); by 1981 it was already up to 60 percent. The contrasts in success with industrialization have been so enormous between trade liberalizing and protectionist countries that the old-fashioned view that protection favors manufacturing in developing countries has lost its appeal.*

Little wonder that it is the Korean model, and not the Indian, that is increasingly being adopted by Thailand, the Philippines, mainland China, and Indonesia. Even smaller wonder that India is now trying to jettison its policies in favor of a more liberal approach generally toward the encouragement of foreign capital. Malaysia, which has benefited for some ten years from running a relatively open and successful economy, seems of late for some strange reason to have been turning in on herself, with doubtlessly damaging effect. If Malaysia has genuinely set out on a changed course, she will be moving in the opposite direction from most of her neighbors.

In any event, these days it is not in the economically dynamic East that the cry for protectionism goes up but in the mighty, though currently relatively sluggish, West.

There is no doubt that despite the empirical and intuitive

evidence of the benefits of free trade, the cause of protectionism is being taken up in the West. Populist politicians who attack the notion of free trade on both sides of the Atlantic—men such as Pat Buchanan (Ross Perot's heir apparent) in America and Sir James Goldsmith in Europe—are attracting to themselves a growing following, not only on the streets and in the saloon bars but in editorial offices, academic common rooms, and legislative debating chambers.

Nor is it just a matter of rhetoric; protectionism over the last twenty years has become a fact of policy. Despite all the to-ings and fro-ings at GATT, nontariff barriers to trade have expanded in number exponentially from the mid-1970s.

Beginning with the highly restrictive multifiber agreement of 1974, orderly marketing and voluntary export restraint agreements have grown apace. By the late 1980s these nontariff barriers (most involving export quotas) covered almost 20 percent of the imports of industrial countries and affected industries as diverse as steel, automobiles, footwear, motorcycles, machine tools, and electronics.

Parallel to this is an increasing use, I would say abuse, in particular by the European Commission, of the antidumping provisions allowed under Article XIX of the GATT rules. These permit a temporary restraint on imports where it can be shown that their prices are manifestly not based upon an economic costing. As was discovered by Patrick Messerlin as long ago as 1987 in a World Bank Publication, the Commission tends to take antidumping applications of member countries virtually at their face value, making little attempt to assess their validity. Once the restrictions have been put in place, far from being temporary, as demanded by GATT, they tend to remain in place even where the exporter has changed his price. Mr. Messerlin concludes: "The EC antidumping procedure . . . involves hundreds of cases, concerns all the important trade partners of the Community and shows increasingly restrictive outcomes. . . . There is a clear tendency for this GATT-honored procedure to generate outcomes embarrassing to GATT principles." This issue was recognized during the Uruguay Round as being significant but was left unresolved in the final agreement.

Whereas the Europeans have tended to focus on new antidumping measures to get around the spirit of GATT, the Americans have tended to make more use of a mixture of countervailing duties and the threat thereof to back up their insistence on so-called "voluntary" export restraints by competitive countries. A recent variant of what has come to be known as "managed trade" is "voluntary import expansion" (VIE). By this means "voluntary" export flows are negotiated by the United States for particular products for which it considers itself to be at an unfair advantage in the importing country. Since 1993 VIEs have been increasingly favored by the Clinton administration as being supportive of U.S. exports, especially to Japan, without apparently harming the progress of world trade. As Douglas Irwin has shown in his booklet "Managed Trade" (AEI Press, 1994), VIEs, backed up as they usually are by threats of import restraint by the U.S. or even tariffs, are an aberration from genuinely free trade and should be treated as another form of protectionism. (The threat of tariffs, for instance on Japanese automobiles, reached a crescendo in Washington in the summer of 1995 when 100 percent tariffs were suggested for certain Japanese makes.)

In the end it all comes to the same thing: the rhetoric of free trade and the concentration on tariff reductions have progressively over the last twenty years been eroded by quantitative restrictions or distortions on trade. Although exporters have often found ways of circumventing these restrictions so that world trade has continued to grow, albeit at a slower pace than before, the protectionist and interventionist pressures are mounting to the point where economic growth is now being seriously threatened, especially in the West, in particular Europe.

Above all, the scramble is on, on both sides of the Atlantic, to set up massive trade blocs that are imagined as trade fortresses from which a defense can be mounted against the attack from the East.

At the heart of the problem—both as a cause and an effect of protectionism—lies the seemingly relentless growth of unemployment in the Western industrialized countries. The phenomenon affects both North America and Europe, though it is more acute in the latter. Average unemployment rates, which were around the 5 percent mark in the United States in the middle 1970s, are currently running at around 7 percent. In the European Union, the comparable figures are 3 percent and 10 percent. In both cases the long-term trend continues upward.

It is true that there has been a cultural shift in the West that has made the growing level of unemployment more acceptable; there is, at least for the time being, apparently a greater acquiescence on the part of those who work that they must pay for those who do not. What is more, the stigma has gone out of not having a job. Europe, in particular, is beset by a new unemployment culture; there, if the head of the household is out of work, it is expected that he or she will pass a good deal of time engaged in activities that have nothing to do with looking for work. In the United States it is still expected, indeed required, of the unemployed that they spend much of their time interviewing or researching in the employment office. In Japan it remains a disgrace to be out of work at all.

Even in Europe, however, the work ethic goes too deep for the rapid rise of those unable to find work not to be a major issue. It is, in these circumstances, natural to look for scapegoats, preferably in some far-off place, where fact and myth can be welded together with impunity. The assumption (based on the curious notion of a static pool of jobs to be shared around the world) is that "somebody out there is taking our jobs." The focus turns easily on the East, where "slave labor" industries are set to ravage Western jobs weighed down with their "civilized" working conditions. This is the thesis of, for instance, James Goldsmith, MEP. "We must have the courage," he says, "entirely to rethink the reasoning by which we believe in the benefits of free trade at world level." Why? "Because there has been a surge in today's world economic system in the number of countries whose manpower costs are a fraction of those which exist in the industrialized world. . . . It is not simply a question of cheaper manpower but of a totally different condition, as if we were being faced with another world or another planet."* Somewhat surprisingly, Goldsmith takes this view while at the same time opposing the development of the European Union.

Forget for a moment that much of the protectionist paraphernalia that Goldsmith advocates is already in place (and has already without doubt acted as a brake on the growth of the world economy and of the job market worldwide). Temporarily forget also that, until recently at least, most of the tough competition faced by the West from the Orient has come from countries with relatively high wage costs, notably Japan but also increasingly Taiwan and South Korea. Ignore for the time being the fact that many

---

*Quoted from *La Piège* (The Trap), in which Yves Messarovitch interviewed Jimmy Goldsmith (1994).

of the handicaps suffered by the West—such as the high social cost of employing people★—have recently been man-made there. (See Figs. 4, 5, and 6.) Let us trace for a moment the direction that the protectionist argument is taking in the West. It goes like this: Since we in the West can no longer compete with the low-cost economies of the East, we must make ourselves self-sufficient so that we do not need to import from the East; we must make ourselves independent. We cannot do this as individual national economies; with the exception of the United States we are too small (to take on such mighty giants as Singapore, Hong Kong, and Taiwan), so we must combine into trading blocs. This will give us two big advantages; first, by enjoying a large home market, our industries will be able to develop economies of scale; second, collectively, we will develop "clout" with which we will be able to make treaties on favorable terms to ourselves with our trading enemies. (It is axiomatic with protectionists that trade is seen not as a process involving a mutuality of interest but as war.)

There used to be a third, rather more respectable, argument for trade blocs, which was, for instance, the overt motivation for Britain's accession to the European Common Market, as it was in 1972: that within the confines of the outer perimeter, there would be scope for the laws of specialization and comparative advantage to work happily according to the classical rules of free trade. Goldsmith's philosophy does indeed hark back to this notion of a trade bloc. Sadly, as we shall see, certainly with respect to

---

★These are especially prevalent in the countries of the European Union. In 1994 nonwage labor "add-on" costs were 16 percent of labor costs in manufactures in the United Kingdom, 24 percent in Germany, and 30 percent in France and Italy.

Fig. 4

GENERAL GOVERNMENT RECEIPTS FROM TAXES AND SOCIAL CONTRIBUTIONS
as Percentage of GDP

	1983			1993		
	Taxes on Income and Wealth (a)	Employers' Social Contributions (b)	Employees' Social Contributions (b)	Taxes on Income and Wealth (a)	Employers' Social Contributions (b)	Employees' Social Contributions (b)
Belgium	19.3	8.1	5.1	16.6	9.8	5.2
Denmark	26.7	0.9	0.9	30.3	0.3	1.3
Germany	12.0	7.5	6.3	11.5	8.0	7.0
Greece	n.a.	n.a.	n.a.	5.2 (c)	4.7 (c)	3.9 (c)
Spain	7.8	9.6	2.1	12.4 (d)	9.3 (d)	2.0 (d)
France	9.0	12.4	5.0	9.2	12.0	6.0
Ireland	13.8	3.6	2.5	15.0 (d)	3.3 (d)	2.3 (d)
Italy	12.4	8.9	2.5	16.2	9.0	2.7
Luxembourg	20.1	6.8	5.8	14.9	6.2	4.9
Netherlands	13.4	8.2	9.2	16.9	3.6	11.5
Austria	11.9	6.6	5.5	12.7	7.3	6.4
Portugal	7.9	6.0	2.5	9.2 (e)	6.4 (e)	3.5 (e)
Finland	n.a.	n.a.	n.a.	16.1	10.4	4.3
Sweden	21.7	12.9	0.0	21.1	13.0	0.4
United Kingdom	15.0	3.5	3.6	12.2	3.6	2.7

(a) Current taxes on income and wealth include taxes on personal income (income from employment, property, etc); taxes on the profits of companies; taxes on the capital or wealth of households: corporate bodies and nonprofit institutions; taxes on lottery, gambling, and betting winnings; and taxes paid by households for the use of vehicles for nonbusiness use.

(b) Social contributions include all payments made by insured persons or their employers to institutions providing social benefits. This table shows general government revenue from social contributions. However, such contributions are payable not only to the State but also to other residents such as insurance companies.

(c) 1989 figures.
(d) 1992 figures.
(e) 1991 figures.

Source: *Taxes and Social Contributions 1982–93*, Eurostat.

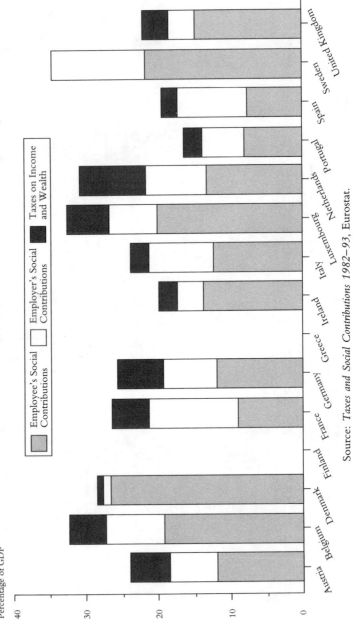

Fig. 5
TOTAL TAX REVENUE AS A PERCENTAGE OF GDP, 1983

Percentage of GDP

Employee's Social Contributions

Employer's Social Contributions

Taxes on Income and Wealth

Source: *Taxes and Social Contributions 1982–93*, Eurostat.

Fig. 6
TOTAL TAX REVENUE AS A PERCENTAGE OF GDP, 1993

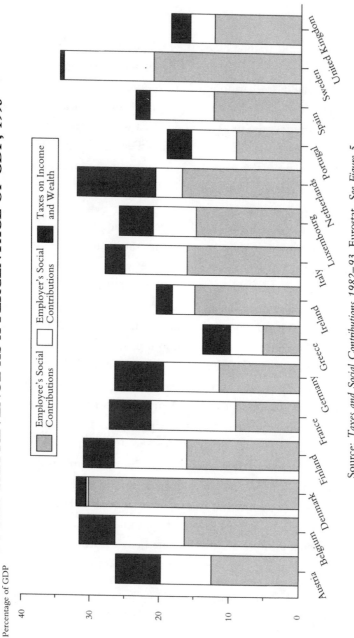

Source: *Taxes and Social Contributions 1982–93*, Eurostat. *See Figure 5.*

the largest of the trading blocs, the European Union,⋆ this motivation and its potential advantages are being increasingly obscured by the demands for harmonization, common social policies, "level playing fields," and of a single economy, which is the essence of a single currency, the insistence on which was the main ingredient of the Maastricht Treaty of 1993, amending the Treaty of Rome. Put another way, the shift has been away from an emphasis on measures to release trade to one of trade restriction in the name of fair play.

The first problem that the European "trade blockers" have is to decide who it is they are really at war with. Goldsmith says at one point, "America seeks to impose world free trade" (sadly, not quite the reality these days). "United, Europe can protect itself." So, in true Gallic tradition, America is reinstated as the enemy. But this does not quite square with the point that seemed to be at the root of Goldsmith's concerns, that we were facing a trading monster whose way of life and whose labor costs were so different from ours that it was "as if he were from another world or another planet." The American economy is not in a different orbit from that of European countries; in many of its sectors it is just more efficient. So the European worry with respect to America is with good old-fashioned competition.

What the European protectionists are in essence saying, at least with respect to America, is that they would rather back the interests of producers than those of consumers and, if a trade war should develop, those of relatively inefficient European businesses against efficient exporters reaching free markets. If the "enemy"

⋆Belgium, Denmark, France, Germany, Greece, Ireland, Italy, Luxembourg, Netherlands, Portugal, Spain, United Kingdom.

is truly in the East, the logic of the European trade blockers should not be to fight the Americans but to team up with them. They had better hurry up, because their counterparts in the United States have firm designs (currently being rebuffed) on forming protective arrangements with the countries of APEC (Asia-Pacific Economic Cooperation). Certainly the countries of NAFTA (the U.S., Canada, and Mexico) already have much stronger trading links with the nations of the Far East than they do with the European Union. In 1994 NAFTA exported 147 billion dollars' worth of goods and imported 235 billion dollars' worth to and from the countries of APEC. The comparable figures for NAFTA trade with the European Union were 126 billion dollars and 113 billion dollars.

I shall deal directly with the whole protectionist argument in Chapter 6, but let me answer straightaway the central notion of the trade blockers that, in order to take on the rest of the world, you need a large home market. A quick answer is to point to the triumphant experience of the small city-states, Hong Kong and Singapore. However, since it is the trade blockers' argument that the real objective is self-sufficiency, this will not quite do. The argument is that certain industries in an all-embracing portfolio will require economies of large-scale production and that in order to achieve these you need a large home market. In a paper approved on 17 May 1995 by the Council of the British Confederation of British Industries, the point was put like this:

> A strong European "home market" is *essential* (my italics) to enhance the EU's international competitiveness and promote competition from within. Only then can the benefits of greater economies of scale, reduced costs, and better choice

and quality be enjoyed by Europe's businesses and citizens alike. Therefore consolidating the Single Market remains *the* business priority.

The first point to make about this is the obvious one: that there is nothing intrinsically special about a home market, unless it is a protected market. What an industry that supposedly requires economies of scale needs is a dynamic market per se, preferably throughout the world. It should not care whether this is defined as "home" or "abroad." All that matters to it is that there should be enough customers to buy its products at prices that give it a good return on its investment. It is important to be clear, therefore, that the argument for large home markets is a dimension of protectionism and has little in itself to do with industrial economics.

The second point to make is that a large amount of the talk about economies of scale has itself been shown to be fallacious. Let us take the parable of IBM. If there was one company in the world that seemed in the 1960s and the 1970s to represent, almost to deify, the notion that to be big was to be invincible, it was International Business Machines. Writing in 1968, Jean-Jacques Servan-Schreiber, the Freud political journalist, marveled at IBM's 5 billion-dollar investment in its 360 series; this, he reminded his readers, was a sum equal to the entire annual space budget of the U.S. government in the middle of a frenetic space race with the Soviet Union. In the second paragraph of his book *The American Challenge* (Hamish Hamilton, 1968), Servan-Schreiber wrote: "Recent efforts by European firms to centralize and merge are due largely to the need to compete with American giants like International Business Machines."

Size and success were seen as self-evidently and inextricably linked together, especially with respect to high-technology industries. The response to the "American penetration of Europe" was of necessity to build organizations of comparable size to take on the Yanks at their own game. In the eighties a variant of this argument came to be applied to meet competition from the Japanese conglomerates.

And yet by the early 1990s the giant IBM was adrift, wallowing in the mire of its own bureaucracy. By July 1994, IBM had plunged in one year from being the world's third most valuable brand name to the bottom of a league table constructed by *Financial World* of 290 brands. So embedded was IBM in its own doctrine of the invincibility of bigness that it took a while for the new chief executive, Lou Gerstner (the first outsider to have been appointed, in March 1993, to that position in the entire history of the company), to fully appreciate what needed to be done. As late as May 1993, Mr. Gerstner was reported as having stopped the breakup of the giant into manageable parts. He was quoted as saying, "The whole of IBM is greater than the sum of its parts." It was not until a year later that concrete evidence began to emerge of a radical reformation, which involved, amongst other things, the licensing to archrival Hitachi of what would previously have been seen as the core process of making microprocessor chips. The penny had dropped even at IBM that the essence of business and of commerce is not bigness but profitability and that the two are by no means the same thing.

The myth that bigness is what counts lingers on; it is central to the thinking of the trade blockers. It is, as I have said, one of two justifications for the creation of a large single market.

There is all the difference in the world between a single market and a free market. It is a distinction that free marketeers on both sides of the Atlantic have been slow to grasp. The reason for this is that each at the outset involves the lowering, if not the abolition, of tariffs between different countries. The objective in each case is, however, very different. The mission of the free marketeer is largely completed once the barriers to trade have been removed. For the trade blocker it marks the starting point for a more profound process. For the free marketeer, differences between countries that have removed their barriers to trade are the very generating force of trade. Without differences there is no reason to swap. For the trade blocker, on the other hand, the aim is not free trade at all. What he wants is to create a new and much larger oneness where size and uniformity are of the essence, to provide scope for general self-sufficiency and, more especially, for the perceived needs of large-scale industry. The free trader is concerned with ensuring that barriers are not only brought down among the designated group of like-minded countries but also between them and the rest of the world. By contrast, one of the instruments by which the trade blocker seeks self-sufficiency is the trade wall built around the single market. For him the process of third-party trade is one of negotiating from a position of strength, which means, rather paradoxically, from behind trade walls. This was precisely how the French government and the European Commission saw matters during the latter stages of the GATT Uruguay Round.

The radically divergent views of the trade blocker and the free marketeer lead each, logically, to contrasting opinions about wider political implications. The free marketeer has a minimalist view of government, whose role he sees essentially as that of allowing the forces of supply and demand to work through as smoothly as possible. Government should as far as possible not intervene between the interests of consumers and producers. In the world of free markets, they have a common interest linked by a mutual requirement that there should be the most efficient possible flow of goods from one to the other. The key to achieving this is the proper working of the price system. Price is the flashpoint of a transaction and should accurately relate to costs. Trouble comes only when prices are distorted and no longer reflect the point at which buyer and seller freely meet and do business. Price distortions can occur for many reasons, and it is the job of government to iron these out. Typically, prices become distorted because of some action the government itself has taken, either in the form of direct intervention or by mismanaging the money supply.

At an international level, and thus at the level of trade, the main distortive action that can be taken by governments over the pricing mechanism is when they restrain the movements of the rate at which currencies exchange against each other. As with any other price, this should merely reflect the relative costs at which different countries produce their goods and services. Part of the free trade answer to those who are fearful of competition from the East is that cost differences should be matched by exchange rate changes until a new equilibrium is reached where free trading again makes sense on each side.★

The trade blocker takes an entirely different view of all this. He spurns the floating exchange as making it impossible for his favored big business to plan ahead "with assurance" and argues that a falling rate of exchange will be demoralizing and inflationary. (It will be so only in the event that more highly priced imports continue to flow in at the same rate as before and that governments print money to accommodate them.) Retreating behind his protective walls, the trade blocker concentrates upon "building up" his own industries. This he does by raising taxes to help finance the industries

---

★Chapter 6 deals in greater detail with the matter, specifically with the pro-free-trade, anti-floating-exchange-rate arguments raised by Judith Shelton in her book *Money Meltdown*.

he considers critical to the policy of self-sufficiency and by pressing on with measures to create a homogeneous single market that satisfies the perceived needs of large companies for the necessary economies of scale. The higher taxes and the bureaucratic regulations necessary to create the single market themselves place more burdens on industry. From the end of the telescope through which the trade blocker views such matters, this necessitates even tougher protectionist measures against marauding cheap-labor-based, or unfairly efficient, outsiders.

The immediate losers in this downward-spiraling process are the taxpayer, the consumer, and the frustrated exporter suffering retaliation from some equally persistent trade blocker in a third country. Sadly, it has been the trade blocker who in the past twenty years has been gaining the upper hand with respect not only to trading philosophy in the West but also to its practice.

The trade bloc with much the longest history and with the sharpest self-image and clearest set of rules is the European Union. An assessment of the psychology, impact, and future of trade blocs must of necessity draw very largely on the European experience. Sufficient historical data now exist for an early assessment to be made of the economic performance of the European experiment. From the point of view of international trade, EU exports have grown over the past twenty years or so by an average annual rate of under 5 percent; this rate is showing signs of slowing down and compares with a comparable rate for the "newly industrialized Asian" (NIA) states of over 10 percent, which is accelerating (Fig. 1). This trade performance has been reflected in recent times by rates of growth in output in Europe of under 3 percent, against an NIA average of some 8 percent per annum.

The comparatively lackluster performance of the European Union (relative to other parts of the world and to the historical experience of some of its constituent countries) currently shows no sign of improving; rather, the reverse is the case. It is largely explained by a lack of competitiveness and by high costs. Many of these have been self-inflicted and recently so. For example, over the last twenty years personal income tax and social security charges have grown in the EU from around 15 percent of GDP in the early 1970s to around 25 percent today (1996). The comparable figures in Japan and the United States are 18 and 20 percent respectively.

As shown in Figs. 7 and 8, general taxation in most Western countries has risen in recent years and is set to continue to rise, in most cases to about 40 percent of GDP. The comparable figure in Communist China is 15 percent. Figs. 4, 5, and 6 indicate the growth in "social contributions" made in the countries of the European Union by employers and employees in industry. In the case of France, for instance, these are now around 20 percent of GDP.

The question is whether by building a trade wall around itself the EU will be able to cocoon its citizens from the effects (I would say "spur") of world competition so that they will be satisfied by a standard of living that is declining relative to that enjoyed in other parts of the world. My guess is that the answer is a clear "no." Even the European Commission, with its proposed "culture" budget of some 1 billion pounds, will not be able to hide from the citizens of Europe what is going on in the rest of the world. Inevitably they will come to resent what they see.

The rise of the trade blockers is particularly surprising when one considers the extraordinary and proven success of Western notions of free trade over many centuries. It is especially ironic, given the thrust of contemporary French thinking on this matter, that it was a group of French philosophers and nobles at the court of Louis XV

Fig. 7

TOTAL TAX REVENUE AS A PERCENTAGE OF GDP

	1980	1993
Australia	28.4	28.7
Austria	41.2	43.6
Belgium	44.4	45.7
Canada	31.6	35.6
China	12.8	15.1 (a)
Denmark	45.5	49.9
Finland	36.9	45.7
France	41.7	43.9
Germany	38.2	39.0
Greece	29.4	41.2
Iceland	29.2	31.3
Ireland	32.4	36.3
Italy	30.2	47.8
Japan	25.4	29.1
Luxembourg	46.0	44.6
Netherlands	45.0	48.0
New Zealand	32.9	35.7
Norway	47.1	45.7
Portugal	28.7	31.4
Spain	24.1	35.1
Sweden	48.8	49.9
Switzerland	30.8	33.2
Turkey	17.9	23.5
United Kingdom	35.3	33.6
United States	29.3	29.7

(a) 1991 figure expressed as a percentage of GNP

Sources: *Revenue Statistics of OECD Member Countries 1965–94; China Statistical Yearbook, 1992.*

in the mid-eighteenth century (some years before the publication of Adam Smith's *Wealth of Nations*) who formalized the view that freedom of trade was part of the law of nature. Adam Smith's

Fig. 8
TOTAL TAX REVENUE AS A PERCENTAGE OF GDP

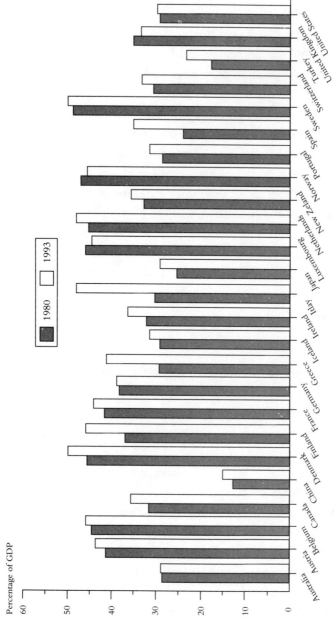

Source: *Revenue Statistics of OECD Member Countries; China Statistical Yearbook, 1992.*

"hidden hand" was a development of this view, which he expressed so elegantly at the beginning of Chapter 2 of *Wealth of Nations*: "This division of labour, from which so many advantages are derived . . . is the necessary, though very slow and gradual, consequence of a certain propensity in human nature . . . the propensity to truck, barter and exchange one thing for another."

It was not so much that Adam Smith and the French philosophers invented this notion of the normalcy of free trade; it was more that it was part of a culture they had inherited over hundreds of years. Its central position in Western philosophy is the single most important reason for the economic success of the West as against the Oriental economies. It carries with it the corollary that to restrict trade is to engage in an unnatural practice.

Perhaps this itself explains why the trade blockers and the protectionists, although undoubtedly currently commanding the heights—certainly in Europe—may yet not win the war. In Europe at least the free traders are reforming, allying themselves to those who are above all concerned about the threat to democracy that the European Union poses in some of its current facets. The free traders are beginning to face off against the trade blockers. The contest is not quite an equal one because in Europe so many of the instruments for protection and centralization are now in place; above all, the new legal system has a momentum of its own, giving it a confidence in its supremacy over the laws of the nation-states. If the trade blockers can but be left alone, all will be theirs; the dynamics of the system they have set up will ensure it. And yet a new mood is sweeping through important parts of the European polity. Parliamentary parties, especially of the center-right, are beginning to gird their loins and to question the newly received wisdom about the benefits of size and of centralization.

★   ★   ★

A BATTLE BETWEEN the two contrasting sets of ideas and interests lies immediately ahead. Indeed, a starting date has been fixed for the grand tournament at which the matter will probably be settled one way or the other. During 1996 the heads of government will begin to reappraise the Treaty of Rome under whose protective shield the trade blockers achieve their current ascendancy. The opportunity will be presented, perhaps for the last time, either to complete the formation of a United States of Europe, which is the logical destination of the European trade blockers, or to pull back and recreate an association of nation-states based on the principles of free trade.

The ramifications of the decisions that will be taken in 1996 about the future shape and philosophical basis of Europe will go far wider than the borders of Europe itself. They will have a bearing not only on future trade patterns per se, but on the stability and security of the world as it enters the twenty-first century.

One reason for this is that trade blocs are not merely restrictive; they are also exclusive. The EU, for instance, is currently conceived to exclude the countries of the former Soviet bloc. If the exclusion proves effective and these countries are denied access to markets for their products, their presently fragile political systems will be further undermined. With respect to Russia and Ukraine, European countries will be faced (not for the first time) with militarily strong but economically disoriented and frustrated powers; the difference from historical precedents will be that each will be armed with nuclear weapons the like of which no country other than the United States will be able to match.

If the trade blockers win, the possibility, still an open one, that

Western-inspired rules of free trade will lead to free governments around the world will have been lost. In order to judge the global effect of this, one only has to consider the threat to world stability of an isolated, dictatorial, nuclear-armed, space-seeking China, which within the next few years may have the highest gross national product on earth. Let me now do just that.

CHAPTER THREE

THE QUESTION
OF SECURITY

I T WOULD BE bad enough from the point of view of the West were the rise of the East merely a question of a growing challenge to the Western liberal ethos or, indeed, just a matter of economic rivalry. The anxiety may turn to genuine dismay, if not fear, when the military dimension is considered. What is then at stake is not only any continuing ability the West may have to contribute toward global peace but its capacity to protect its own vital interests.

The problem is that the West's military superiority is ebbing by the day. Several distinct factors are contributing to this process. Among these are: the dramatic and conscious arming of the Asian countries themselves; the worldwide and decreasingly controllable spread of nuclear weapons; the growing tensions between Europe and the United States resulting in a loss of cohesion and disorientation within NATO; the restoration of undemocratic regimes in much of the former Soviet Empire; and the growth of ethnic tensions, especially in Central Europe.

One of the most difficult of these to measure is the speed with which Asia, and in particular China, is arming itself. What is clear is that a massive modernization of China's four-million-strong armed forces is under way. Particular attention is being given to the navy, which now boasts one of the largest submarine fleets in the world; many of these boats are being armed with nuclear warheads. This fleet is developing a "blue water" role and is increasingly encountering the maritime forces of the United States. A particularly awkward incident occurred in October of 1994, when the U.S. aircraft carrier *Kitty Hawk*, tracking Chinese submarine movements in the Yellow Sea, was challenged by Chinese military aircraft scrambled for the purpose. This was accompanied by public Chinese warnings that in the future their forces could not be relied upon to "stand off."

The London-based Institute for Strategic Studies has indicated that whereas defense budgets in the United States declined between 1990 and 1993 by some 11 percent, the comparable known figure in China was a rise of some 20 percent, with similar increases in Taiwan and South Korea. For Indonesia and Japan, the increase was over 30 percent. Vietnam, for which no comparable figures are available in the West, is known to have almost three-quarters of a million men under arms. Another way of looking at the arms buildup in Asia is that, according to published figures, Japan, China, Taiwan, and South Korea together spent nearly 70 billion dollars on defense in 1993; this was more than double the Russian defense budget that year. What is more, these published figures are likely to be highly conservative. Actual figures for China, for instance, may be higher by as much as 300 percent. Some estimates put spending in 1995 on the Chinese People's Liberation Army at 53 billion dollars, which, if true, would place it at a level only just behind that of the United States.

Seen through China's eyes, this massive buildup of arms has no necessarily sinister implications for the West: having in November 1993 become a net importer of oil, and anticipating oil imports of some 3 million barrels a day by the year 2000, China can claim to be protecting her new interests. In the near future the focus of her attention may be directed against other Asian powers rather than against the West. This is clearly true, with respect to her claims over the Spratley Islands and her increasingly frequent naval confrontations with the Philippines. Most dramatically, there is China's undistinguished and renewed threat to Taiwan.

What is indisputable is that the Western powers carry rapidly diminishing clout in the China Seas. The lowering of the Union Jack over Government House in Hong Kong in June 1997 will have a symbolism for Western military power wider than that of merely bringing down the final curtain on the British Empire, and the decline of Western military potency has wider and deeper causes than that of the rising military might of the Orient.

There is first the issue of the spread of nuclear weapons. Since the fall of the Berlin Wall, the superpowers have no longer been able to check the nuclear pretensions of either their friends or their enemies. The United States has begun to lose control over the capitalist states of East Asia. More seriously, the withdrawal of Soviet protection has prompted Iraq and North Korea to intensify their nuclear programs. The breakup of the USSR brought four nuclear powers into existence where there had previously been one; it also threw hundreds of nuclear scientists onto the international nuclear labor market.

With the two-power equilibrium destroyed, countries have gained a new incentive to maintain, extend, or develop nuclear weapons. Nuclear proliferation has become a self-driven process as states are forced to counterbalance the capability of nuclear-armed neighbors. Thus, President Kim Young Sam has announced

NUCLEAR STATES: Summary of the Position

"Official" Nuclear Powers

UNITED STATES

8,750 total operational warheads as of July 1995[1]; 7,770 strategic warheads in stockpile as of January 1995[2]. The difference between these two figures is mainly, but not entirely, attributable to the existence of around 1,000 non-strategic warheads. These were estimated at 1,150 in July 1995, but 350 consisted of submarine-launched cruise missiles no longer carried at sea.[3]

UNITED KINGDOM

Numbers of warheads are not announced, but an authoritative estimate is 250–300 at January 1995[4]; around one hundred of these are WE-177 bombs currently assigned to a sub-strategic role with the Tornado aircraft, but these will all be withdrawn once the third Trident submarine becomes operational in around 1998, at which point Trident will assume both the strategic and the non-strategic roles. At present the new Trident warheads are gradually replacing Polaris warheads in the stockpile; it is possible that when the process has been completed and all the Polaris warheads dismantled there may be significantly fewer than two hundred warheads in the operational stockpile.[5]

---

[1] Natural Resources Defense Council figure, published in the *Bulletin of Atomic Scientists*, July–August 1995.
[2] *SIPRI Yearbook 1995*, p328.
[3] *Bulletin of Atomic Scientists*, July–August 1995, 79.
[4] *SIPRI Yearbook 1995*, 327.
[5] *The United Kingdom and Nuclear Weapons*, Research Paper 95/101, House of Commons Library, 12.

FRANCE

"Just over 500 warheads" in January 1995.[6]

CHINA

Figures are especially uncertain and it is not known precisely which aircraft types are nuclear capable or whether a type with tactical range is still in service. SIPRI estimates a total of 300 strategic warheads, consisting of approximately 150 air-borne, 110 land-based and 24 submarine-launched.[7] Past estimates have put the tactical warhead stockpile also at around 150, making a warhead total of 450.[8]

RUSSIA/CIS

The last remaining warheads are due to be returned to the Russian Federation from Ukraine and Belarus during 1996. It is not believed that either of these states could launch the weapons independently of Russia. All nuclear warheads have now been removed from Kazakhstan. The numbers of warheads still to be removed are estimated as follows:

Belarus: 18 single-warhead SS-25 ICBMs plus spare warheads. These were originally expected to be removed by the end of 1995, but the movements were halted by President Lukashenka because of his interest in a possible re-union of Russia and Belarus. The withdrawal is still scheduled to be completed by the end of 1996, but this could be renegotiated since START I does not require the process to be completed before 2001.

---

[6] *SIPRI Yearbook 1995*, p327.
[7] *SIPRI Yearbook 1995*, 333.
[8] *Arms Control Reporter*, 611.E.O.6.

Ukraine: The number of warheads declared under START I was 1,664 in 1994 (around 1,000 associated with ICBMs, the remainder mainly cruise missiles to be launched from strategic bombers).[9] Warheads have been returned to Russia at a steady rate and by September 1995 it was estimated that 700 had already gone, leaving under 1,000. All warheads are due to have been removed to Russia by mid-1996.[10]

The total number of strategic warheads held by the Russian Federation (including those still deployed in Ukraine and Belarus) was put at 7,888 on 1 June 1995.[11] Numbers of tactical warheads are unknown and estimates vary between 6,000 and 13,000.[12]

"Unofficial" Nuclear Powers

ISRAEL

Of the various states which have been described as "undeclared", "threshold" or "suspected" nuclear states, only one, Israel, is firmly believed to possess warheads in a near-operational state. The number is unknown, but SIPRI estimates 55–99 on the basis of the known plutonium stock.[13] IISS estimates "up to 100" warheads.[14]

INDIA

India has tested a nuclear device once, in 1974, has declined to join the Non-Proliferation Treaty and is known to have a missile development program. While there are occasional rumors that India is in a position to make warheads operational at short notice and

[9] *Arms Control Reporter*, 611.E-Russia.7 and *The Military Balance 1995–96*, 100, 285.
[10] *Bulletin of Atomic Scientists*, September/October 1995, 61.
[11] *The Military Balance 1995–96*, 285.
[12] *The Arms Control Reporter*, 611.E-Russia.7.
[13] *SIPRI Yearbook 1995*, 327.
[14] *The Military Balance 1995–96*, 136.

might hold another nuclear test, or even openly declare itself a nuclear weapon state, these have been firmly denied[15] and neither SIPRI nor IISS currently regards it as such.

Pakistan, Iran, and North Korea appear to have clandestine nuclear weapon aspirations and have made some advances in acquiring the necessary technologies and stockpiles of fissionable materials, but none appears to possess warheads in operational or near-operational condition. Estimates vary as to how long it would take them to achieve nuclear weapon capability from their present position, but this would probably take several years in each case and all three are under heavy international pressure (especially from the United States) to hold back. Iraq was in a similar position before the Gulf War and the subsequent UN program to destroy all of its weapons of mass destruction.[16]

Current and former ''problem'' states

Brazil, Argentina and South Africa have all been interested in nuclear weapons programs in the past for reasons of regional deterrence, but have now abandoned such aspirations and have acceded to international treaties and safeguard regimes.

Algeria, Syria, and Libya have all been suspected of having longer term nuclear weapon aspirations and of having developed their civil nuclear activities with this in mind, but there is no hard evidence that they have made any significant progress.

Many other states have civil nuclear programs and advanced technology which would allow them to become nuclear weapon states quite rapidly if their governments wanted this. There are several states in

---

[15] *The Economist*, 23 December 1995.
[16] *The Extension of the Non-Proliferation Treaty*, Research Paper 94/99, House of Commons Library, October 1994.

the Far East in this category which, it is believed, might feel obliged to change their non-nuclear status in the event of North Korea obtaining a nuclear weapon capability—Japan, South Korea, and Taiwan are most frequently mentioned in this context.

that South Korea "would not sit idle" if the North succeeded in developing the bomb, while Taiwan has also indicated that it would not remain undefended if an East Asian nuclear arms race began.

In addition to the 20,000 nuclear warheads in the former USSR, there are an estimated 850 tons of plutonium and enriched uranium (a single atom bomb requires little more than 15 kilograms of uranium). Russia, Ukraine, Kazakhstan, Belarus, Uzbekistan, and Kyrgyzstan are all believed to possess uranium enrichment facilities.

On 10 August 1994, German police arrested a Colombian and two Spaniards in Munich carrying plutonium on a flight from Moscow. It emerged that they were involved in a four-kilogram deal worth 250 million dollars. A few days later, a German was arrested selling plutonium in Bremen. The result of these seizures was to spark panic in the West about the widespread dissemination of nuclear technology. But these arrests were nothing new. There had been evidence of nuclear smuggling since at least the beginning of 1992, when just under a kilogram of radioactive uranium dioxide was found in a hotel safe in Szazanug, Hungary. At the time of the Munich and Bremen seizures, groups of Poles, Slovaks, Germans, Czechs, and Pakistanis were under investigation for trafficking in nuclear material, and a large number of Western businessmen had reported approaches made to them by Russian and Ukrainian officials.

There are few technical difficulties in developing a nuclear bomb.

It is frankly miraculous that the spread has been contained as success-fully as it has over the last fifty years. Israel and South Africa provide incontestable evidence that a bomb can be developed by any modern state with the political will to do so and that it can be done with a large measure of secrecy. These two countries faced arms embargoes, trade boycotts, regular inspection, and international sus-picion, and nonetheless succeeded in building nuclear weapons. South Africa became capable of producing weapons-grade uranium and, despite one hundred and fifteen separate inspections, had six bombs by 1990; Israel has up to ninety-eight. Any reasonably industrialized country can acquire the know-how to build a bomb, given sufficient time. Concealment is easier if the uranium enrich-ment method is used rather than the extraction of plutonium from a reactor. Israel used plutonium, South Africa uranium. North Korea has the potential for both.

If the material necessary to build a bomb is readily available, so too are the scientists with the requisite knowledge. This also has been true since the end of the Cold War. In an interview with the *Thüringer Allgemeine* as early as December 1991, Manfred Wörner, the former secretary general of NATO, declared:

> *The uncontrolled proliferation of weapons of mass destruction is one of our greatest concerns. And it relates not only to the proliferation of weapons, but also to the dissemination of technology through a "brain drain" of specialists. I mean not only nuclear weapons experts but also experts in chemical and biological weapons. Some of them will become unemployed. In some cases, their social condi-tions will become so poor that they will prefer to travel to another country to make a living. The de facto means of countering prolifera-tion are still limited.*

So limited, indeed, that four years after Mr. Wörner spoke these words, the West is no closer to solving the problem. According to Soviet intelligence's former chief technician, Professor V. Mikhailov, 100,000 people were employed in the Soviet nuclear program, of whom 10,000 to 15,000 had "access to classified information" and 1,000 to 3,000 held "vital secrets." While most of these technicians were "patriots, responsible people," Professor Mikhailov admitted that "a few adventurists" had sought work abroad. Former Soviet technicians are now believed to be employed in Iraq, Libya, and Syria, as well as Algeria, which is building a reactor with Chinese assistance.

The United States, long the most determined upholder of nonproliferation, appears to be abandoning its uncompromising stance on the issue. Whether through a failure of will or because of simple pragmatism, the U.S. is edging toward a position that regards a certain level of nuclear arms in the world as tolerable. A recent American initiative involved selling F-16 bombers to Pakistan as an incentive for Pakistan not to extend its existing nuclear program by acquiring M-11 missiles. The initiative was viewed with understandable dismay in India, since the F-16s are known to be Pakistan's proposed vehicle for the delivery of its existing nuclear bombs.

William Clark Jr., former U.S. secretary of state for Asian and Pacific Affairs, has warned of the effects that this tacit policy shift could have: "Surely the strange folks who inhabit Pyongyang have not missed the new 'a few are OK' approach to Pakistan regarding nuclear weapons. If they had, Defense Secretary William Perry spelled it out for them on his return trip from the states of the former Soviet Union: 'Our policy right along has been orientated to keep North Korea from getting a significant nuclear weapons capacity.'" (*International Herald Tribune*, 27 April 1994).

Some Western commentators have concluded that a nuclear free-for-all is now inevitable, and that the West's optimum course of action is simply to arm its allies so as to create a standoff: South Korea should be armed to balance the North, Ukraine to deter the Russians, and so on. Voices are even being raised to question the value of maintaining the 1968 Non-Proliferation Treaty.

Another factor undermining confidence in Western military powers, in addition to the spread of nuclear weapons, is the resurfacing of ethnic and national tension. With the dissolution of the supranationalist creed of Soviet Communism, the bond that had artificially held together the different nations of the Soviet empire melted away. Most of the current nationality-based disputes have broken out in the former eastern bloc—Bosnia, Macedonia, and the Caucasus being prime examples. This has led some commentators to a mistaken analysis of the problem: the view of Communism's supranationalism as one of its compensating features. By elevating ideology over national allegiances, the argument goes, Communism subdued the ethnic disputes that are now claiming so many thousands of lives.

This is a quite false diagnosis of the situation in the former eastern bloc. For one thing, Communism often employed the rhetoric of supranationalism in order to mask the dominance of one particular national group: Russians in the USSR, Serbs in Yugoslavia, Han Chinese in China. For another, it relied on the harsh control of a police state, without which the aspiration for nationhood of the subject peoples could not have been suppressed. The notion that the antinationalism of Communism could easily be divorced from its totalitarianism is highly questionable.

The real cause of the conflicts in the old eastern bloc today is not nationalism but its precise opposite: a determination not to recognize people's right to be governed by their compatriots. The war in the Balkans began when the Yugoslav government refused to relinquish its right to govern Slovenia and Croatia and sent its largely Serbian army north to enforce its writ. In the Commonwealth of Independent States (CIS),★ most of the current national conflicts have their origins in the random border changes and population movements of the Soviet period—Khrushchev's whimsical decision to award Russian-populated Crimea to Ukraine, or Stalin's policy of deporting whole peoples to Central Asia as punishment for collaborating with the Nazis.

The destabilization of Central and Eastern Europe has been aggravated by the return to power in several countries of former Communists. They now hold power, in one guise or another, in Latvia, Lithuania, Poland, Slovakia, Hungary, Serbia, Romania, Bulgaria, and several states of the CIS. The former apparatchiks differ in their approaches and methods. In Romania they have retained power consistently since 1989. In Lithuania the renamed Party of Democratic Socialism succeeded by tarring its opponents as KGB collaborators. In Hungary, the Communist government is largely composed of clever young technocrats. In Poland it relies heavily on the support of protectionist farmers. In Serbia the Communists have appropriated the rhetoric of extreme and violent nationalism.

It is possible, however, to identify some common features in the return of the old *nomenklatura*. One is the retention by Communist sympathizers after 1989 of control over such key institutions as the press, the police, and the security services. Working in partnership with the renamed Communists, the security forces have been instrumental in hamstringing the reform process. In Slovakia, the

---

★Armenia, Azerbaijan, Belarus, Kazakhstan, Kyrgyzstan, Moldova, the Russian Federation, Tajikistan, Turkmenistan, Ukraine, Uzbekistan.

State Security (StB) threw its support behind Vladimir Meciar's Communist government, whose first action after victory was to call a halt to the purge of Communist agents and informers. In Lithuania, the KGB was almost certainly responsible for producing mysterious documents on the eve of the election that "proved" that several prominent supporters of the anti-Communist Sajudis movement were on their list of informers. (Many Communist intelligence agencies maintained lists of potential informers without the knowledge of those whose names appeared on them.) In Romania, the Securitate, now renamed the Romanian Intelligence Service, has engaged in telephone tapping and surveillance of government opponents, and has coordinated many of the acts of violence against students and others opposed to Ion Iliescu's apparatchik government. One Western expert on security has summarized the situation in the eastern bloc:

Communism as an ideology is dead. No-one in the old Soviet Bloc (or in China or Cuba for that matter) believes in the ideals of egalitarianism any more, if they ever did. But people and institutions shaped by the cynicism of Communism still abound. In much of Eastern Europe, and throughout the old Soviet Union, with the partial exception of the Baltic States, officials trained under the old order hold the reins of power. This is nowhere more true than in the fields of intelligence and national security.*

The persistence of the ancien régime in these countries is as much based on economic as it is on political factors. Economic reform has strengthened rather than damaged the hold on power

---

*Mark Almond, *Still Serving Secretly: Soviet Bloc Spies under New Masters* (IEDSS, 1993).

of the old elites. The main reason for this is that in the initial stages of marketization, those who did best out of the old order were in the strongest position to profit from privatization. Studies in Poland and Hungary have revealed an astonishing overlap between the top *nomenklaturists* of the old era and the top business executives of today. Playing on their connections with former Communist colleagues now in government, these new entrepreneurs profit from cheap loans, monopolies, rigged privatizations, and insider dealing. In a not untypical case, Ireneusz Sekula, a deputy prime minister of Communist-era Poland, was appointed head of the customs office just in time to save his trading company from bankruptcy. The pace at which former members of the nomenklatura reemerge in Poland is likely to increase now that the Presidency is back in the hands of the Communist Party.

The former Communists are, in particular, able to make use of their past connections with the KGB and its client services. In most of the CIS, much of the military and high technology industries remain directly or indirectly under state control. The KGB's switch from military to economic espionage allows it to promote the success of companies in friendly hands, further distorting the reform process. The apparatchik class not only administers and directs Western aid money but is actively involved in the process of selling monopolies and concessions.

With their own living standards failing to improve in flagrantly rigged markets, it is little wonder that the electorates of Eastern Europe and the CIS have lost their enthusiasm for capitalism. The former Communists have succeeded in wrecking the economic reform program so as to enrich themselves; they have subsequently reaped the electoral reward as people wrongly blame the West for their economic problems.

As well as proving a hindrance to the spread of Western values, the return of the former Communists constitutes a general threat to international stability. Robbed of the ideology that once justified their occupation of high office, many Communists have turned instead to the rhetoric of vicious and illiberal nationalism. Coming from the ideological background of Soviet Communism, the post-Communists neither understand nor care for the rational, civic patriotism of the Western tradition. The nationalism of Slobodan Milosevic in Serbia, of Meçiar in Slovakia, or Iliescu in Romania is a unique product of East European authoritarian Communism, difficult to classify as being either far "left" or far "right." It is distinguished by a fear of Western capitalist domination and of fifth columnists within: national minorities, Jews, Freemasons, or Gypsies. The tone is reminiscent of some of Stalin's speeches: denunciations of "traitors, fascists, criminals and counter-revolutionaries" (labels traditionally attached to the democratic opposition). Newspapers favorable to these politicians often carry stories of attempted CIA infiltration and occasionally descend into wild conspiracy theories about Western-Jewish plots to control the world.

The reemergence of the old *nomenklatura* has been facilitated by Western policy, and in particular by the trade policy of the European Union. Swayed by the naked selfishness of its agricultural, steel, and textile interests, the EU has imposed tariffs on the Central and Eastern European countries that surpass anything seen during the Cold War. The emerging democracies, struggling to rediscover their European heritage, have found that the free market reforms the EU urged upon them have led directly to the EU's closing its markets to their goods.

This unsatisfactory state of affairs was a theme I took up in a speech in Prague in May 1994: "One can only sympathize with the bewilderment of Eastern Europe's trade ministers at the EU's attitude. It lectures them on the merits of free trade while closing its markets and dumping its own surpluses upon them. They undertook rigorous reforms to liberalize key sectors of their industry and agriculture, all in the name of Europe, and now find themselves penalized for their very success."

Without full trade opportunities, the economies of the newly capitalist states were unable to take off properly, exacerbating the unemployment caused by the first jolt of economic reform and heightening political tension. EU tariffs provided a focus for much latent anti-Western hostility in Eastern Europe, and the old *nomenklatura* was able to exploit popular anger as part of its campaign to regain power. On 16 September 1993, for example, the Polish Peasant Party, led by Waldemar Pawlak astonished commentators by sweeping into power in coalition with the Communists on a platform of nationalism and hostility to the EU. The centerpiece of its campaign had been a demand for reciprocal trade barriers against EU goods.

The West made, and continues to make, some attempt at restitution through its aid policy, but aid to the former Soviet bloc tends to find its way into numbered Swiss bank accounts or else ends up financing neo-Communist election campaigns. Being essentially condition free, Western aid does nothing to promote the root-and-branch reform its recipients urgently need.

Both the European Union and the G-7 (Group of Seven)★ maintain massive financial aid programs in Eastern Europe and Russia, totaling tens of billions of dollars. Failure to link this assistance to specific political and economic reforms carries high risks—nowhere more so than in Russia.

The likely stability and political orientation of Russia is clearly

★United States, Canada, Britain, France, Germany, Italy, Japan.

important to an assessment of the prospects for a Western-sponsored equilibrium in the coming years. Russia remains a colossal military superpower, its conventional and nuclear forces intact.

Even the most cursory examination of the facts suggests treating with some skepticism any idea that the Russian reform process is now a fait accompli. Ever since the Russian parliamentary elections, Western politicians have tended to speak of the need to consolidate President Yeltsin's position so as to guard against the possibility that Russia might fall into the hands of an extremist in the mold of Vladimir Zhirinovsky. Yet this attitude rather complacently assumes that a democratic and peaceful future is secure as long as the current regime remains in control.

The truth is that, just as the Soviet Union inherited many of its geopolitical and strategic imperatives from imperial Russia, so today's Russian rulers cannot ignore the lessons of Soviet policy. Despite their economic calamity, the Russian leaders are determined to preserve Russia's inherited status as a superpower and the only plausible rival to the United States. Russian defense spending has increased to 7.4 percent of GDP from 4 percent in 1992, while Boris Yeltsin refuses to abandon the idea of an arms race with the United States, declaring in 1993 that "what they have, we must have." Yeltsin's current policy toward Cuba is some indication of a "business as usual" attitude toward the West. By terms of an agreement made between Yeltsin and Fidel Castro in 1992, Russian electronic surveillance of the United States continues on the island, as, in return, does her economic assistance to the Castro regime, mainly through the sale of oil to Cuba at subsidized prices.

When the Soviet Union collapsed, the Communist Party was put on trial. Not so with the KGB. It was merely rechristened as the Russian Intelligence Service and was not subjected to any judicial inquiry (let alone public scrutiny). Its officers and its methods were left undisturbed. It is hardly likely that lifelong KGB officers will have suddenly reversed their ideological beliefs and strategic assumptions.

There is growing evidence that hard-line army officers are holding increasing influence over the Yeltsin administration. This certainly would explain Russian policy in Chechnya. It may also account for recent reversals in Russian attitudes toward the Baltic states; when the reformed Communists won the parliamentary election in Lithuania, Russia halted its troop withdrawal from Latvia and Estonia.

The Russian state has declared itself responsible for the 25 million Russians beyond its borders in the former USSR. It is fighting openly for ethnic Russians in Moldova, and scarcely troubles to disguise its policy of fomenting unrest among the Russians of the Crimea and Eastern Ukraine.

Various treaties now give Russia a strong interest in the foreign and economic policies of the affiliated Central Asian republics, while Russian troops are active in the region "combating Islamic fundamentalism." The Russian army continues, as if nothing has changed, to defend the old Soviet Union's southern border under an agreement with the Tajik government. Russian tanks on occasion have even been seen flying the Soviet hammer and sickle pendant from their turret tops as they maneuver about these southern states. The hammer and sickle was also much in evidence in the parade in Red Square on 7 May 1995 to mark the anniversary of the end of the war in Europe. The emergence of the Communists as the largest party in the duma, in the 1995 elections was another straw in the wind.

Russian foreign policy is at its most aggressive in the Caucasian region. Russian involvement in Chechnya is merely the most visible recent example. The Russian army has been involved in supplying arms to secessionist groups in Georgia, as well as to the factions that opposed the elected anti-Communist leader Zviad Gamsakhurdia. Both sides in the dispute between Armenia and Azerbaijan have received military assistance from the Russians. In all these cases, the escalation of the fighting, abetted by the Russians, eventually led to an agreement to allow Russian "peacekeepers" into the area. A Russian military presence has thus been reestablished, and the Caucasian republics have been prevented from leaving the CIS. (Georgia's secession was reversed by President Gamsakhurdia's successor, the former senior KGB officer and Soviet foreign minister Eduard Shevardnadze, who assumed power when Gamsakhurdia was overthrown in an armed coup).

This is the country into which the West is pouring economic aid; this the regime to which Western leaders look as the guarantor of security in the region. In the other ex-Soviet republics there is anger at the way the West appears to acknowledge a semilegitimate Russian sphere of influence. Many Ukrainian leaders have complained that Europe and the United States appear to regard their independent existence as transient and irritating. It is little wonder that the West has been slow to persuade Ukraine to dismantle its nuclear weapons. The claim by the West that its own nuclear deterrent was responsible for forty years of world peace does not fully square with the view that Ukraine should abandon its nuclear arms while faced with an unstable and expansionist neighbor that has never fully reconciled itself to Ukrainian independence.

After the Cold War, the former adversaries held dozens of ceremonies and produced hundreds of declarations hailing a new era of cooperation. Few of these magniloquent documents, however, contained specific agreements on new security arrangements. The only one that did so was the Conventional Armed Forces in Europe treaty, which was signed on 20 November 1990 and which entered into force on 9 November 1992. Based on the principle of allowing the minimum military force necessary for self-defense, the treaty not only placed upper limits on the armed forces that each signatory might maintain but also specified where these forces should be deployed. In the absence of any other agreements, this treaty (and a protocol attached to it setting limits on manpower) became the cornerstone of the post–Cold War security edifice. When the situation in the Caucasus escalated, Russia informed the other signatories that it would need to violate the provisions of the treaty in order to transfer a number of troops south as "peacekeepers." NATO failed to dig its heels in, and Russia succeeded in abrogating the one treaty that should have guaranteed the security of the new order.

With such examples of the West's lack of resolution, it is hardly surprising that many in the former Soviet bloc talk of appeasement. There is particular anger in Poland, Hungary, and the Czech Republic that the West has allowed Russia a substantial voice in the question of NATO enlargement.

The West's reaction to the various crises of the post–Cold War world has shown a common thread of irresolution. It has assisted the ex-Communists in their return to power; it has come to support a possibly unstable and certainly domineering Russian government; it has exacerbated the problem of ethnic violence by its insistence on the sanctity of borders. These foreign policy failures are indications of a lack of a coherent agenda in Europe and America. During the Cold War, the West's foreign policy was driven by one overriding objective: the need to preserve the Western democracies from the Communist menace. Its current fumblings and contradictions stem from a failure not so much of nerve as of faith in its own values.

Perhaps the most damning example of the effect of this lack of a clear objective in the West is its response to the crisis in the former Yugoslavia. It is difficult to think of any international event in which the countries of Western Europe have displayed such grotesque incompetence as in the breakup of Yugoslavia. In the Muslim world it is widely believed that the atrocities carried out in Bosnia are part of a deliberate Western policy, a campaign in which the European Union aligned itself with a vicious brand of Eastern Orthodox militancy. The truth—that there is no conspiracy, merely a succession of stupefying mistakes—appears incredible.

The West began its response to the crisis by insisting that it would not countenance anything that might threaten "the integrity of Yugoslavia." This was an error of which the Bush administration was as guilty as the governments of the European Union, but it was the European Union that decided to assume responsibility for the resolution of Yugoslavia's difficulties.

As might be expected, the EU took the line that federal unions must be a more advanced form of government than nation-states. It made clear that its program of economic aid to Yugoslavia depended on the maintenance of political unity, and that the constituent Yugoslav republics would be denied individual entry into the EU. Thus encouraged, the Yugoslav government ordered its army into Slovenia and Croatia. Never mind that the West was effectively backing a Serbian administration in the hands of Communist authoritarians; or that in so doing it was brushing aside the clearly expressed democratic will of the Slovenes and Croats for self-government. By its initial refusal to recognize the breakaway republics and by its imposition of an arms embargo, the EU gave the Serbs an overwhelming political and military advantage. The West was, in effect, intervening on the side of Serbia.

In time it became clear that no outside power could prevent the self-determination of the Croats and Slovenes and, having dispatched the Badinter Commission to evaluate their viability as nations, the European Union was forced to recognize their de facto independence. The Badinter Commission also recommended the recognition of Macedonia on the same criteria, but Greek objections prevented this. So instead, the EU made the calamitous error of recognizing Bosnia-Herzegovina. Bosnia-Herzegovina could no more be held together artificially than could Yugoslavia, and for the same reason: no ethnic group constituted an overall majority. But the EU had learned nothing from its mistakes and clung to the demand that Bosnia must remain united and sovereign, proposing various schemes for power sharing and confederation. Even this policy was bungled in its implementation. As Serbian troops committed atrocity after atrocity, the West responded with finger-wagging resolutions and interminable conferences while denying the Bosnia army the means to defend itself. In response to the criticism that Europe was allowing aggression to be rewarded, EU foreign ministers argued that the conflict in Bosnia was a civil war in which there were "no front lines." The fact was that the Serbian front line was visibly advancing day by day.

Western policy was punctuated by scenes that would, in other circumstances, have been comic: Jacques Poos of Luxembourg solemnly informed Slovenia in 1991 that it was too small to exist as a country; Uffe Elleman-Jensen and Helmut Kohl entered the session of the 1992 EU Lisbon summit devoted to Bosnia with minitelevisions to watch the European soccer final.

Not until late August 1995, some five years after the inception of these catastrophic events during which hundreds of thousands of lives were lost and untold misery suffered, did the West finally respond in force.

The consequences of Western policy in the former Yugoslavia may come to haunt Europe for years to come. Any peaceful world order must rest on the assumption that aggression will be punished. Yet in Bosnia and Croatia, the Serbs were able to carve out a territory for themselves with naked belligerence, attacking civilian populations, cleansing areas of their non-Serb inhabitants, firing with impunity on UN soldiers. Once lost, the principle that aggression will not be rewarded will prove extremely difficult to reassert. Weak and confused signals are being sent eastward.

Moreover, the West's policy in Yugoslavia has damaged its credibility, perhaps irreparably, in Eastern Europe and the Muslim world. It has now become unrealistic for the West to seek arms reductions from any country with a potentially aggressive neighbor. The idea that there might be some new world order enforceable by NATO and the United Nations has been seriously undermined. Countries are beginning to look to their own defenses, knowing that they are without the superpower support for which they might once have hoped. In the Islamic world, the standing of America and Western Europe could hardly be lower. The West's indifference to the Bosnian Muslims is contrasted by politicians and commentators with the massive military operation launched against Saddam Hussein. Westernizers in Islamic countries have complained that their position is weaker than ever. When the fundamentalists argue that the West is guilty of double standards, that is arbitrarily withholds its treasured "human rights" from Muslims, the moderates cannot answer them.

As if all this were not enough, the West may be creating a

more direct threat to itself in the Balkans. Whatever the eventual outcome of Dayton treaty, the repercussions are bound to be long term and severe. If one thing can be said with certainty about the settlement that finally emerges, it is that large numbers of Slavs will refuse to accept it. Hundreds of thousands of people have been uprooted, with no real prospect of returning to their homes. On all sides, the West is regarded with degrees of hostility. The European Union in particular and the West in general may have succeeded in creating a Palestine on its doorstep.

In the wake of the Balkan affair, the Atlantic Alliance is in danger of becoming the first casualty of Western post–Cold War disorientation. A supremely successful organization for half a century, NATO's effectiveness relied on the clarity and certainty of its function. People with only the vaguest knowledge of international politics were familiar with the central pledge of the North Atlantic Treaty: that an attack on any signatory would be treated as an attack on all.

I have identified in this chapter the new threats to Western security that have followed from the end of the Cold War: the rise of China, nuclear proliferation, the spread of ethnic conflict, the emergence of neo-Communism, instability in Russia. Can NATO ever provide a shield against these oblique and indirect menaces as it did against the T-72s once massed on its borders? There is certainly no technical difficulty: the North Atlantic Treaty specifically allows for preemptive and out-of-area action to neutralize a threat to a signatory's security, and many of the causes of instability mentioned involve the violation of United Nations provisions. Nor does NATO, while the United States is a member, lack the military capacity for out-of-area action. The Rapid Reaction Corps of the Allied Command in Europe (ACE) comprises 7 percent of the Alliance's disposable forces ready for immediate deployment in the ACE area. The corps is under British command and contains a disproportionate number of British troops. It aims to be able to dispatch up to four divisions to any sector of the ACE region within fourteen days. The question is not one of military capability but of political will. If NATO would not act against a serious challenge to the stability of Europe in Yugoslavia (which lay directly on NATO borders), will it ever move to anticipate future threats to Western security? If it is not prepared to adopt a broader and more farsighted function, NATO will truly have lost its raison d'être, and the West will have lost the one vehicle that might have guaranteed the security of the new world order. As Senator Richard Lugar has said, NATO risks going out of business if it does not go "out of area."

The notion that NATO faces no obvious challenges could not be more mistaken. Take for a start the question of eastward enlargement. The extension of NATO into Central and Eastern Europe is the one definite way to ensure the stability of a region threatened by unstable borders and bubbling ethnic tensions. It is also the only way to prevent a large part of the European continent from falling once again to Russian imperialism. NATO membership would give a powerful boost to the reformist and pro-Western parties in the region, undoing much of the damage wrought by the reformed Communists who now hold power in so many states. The arguments that justified the creation of NATO in the first place apply with no less validity to the nations of Eastern Europe, which today have cause to fear for their security.

Yet, despite the loud and articulate pleas of many East European politicians, there has been almost no progress toward security integration. The Partnership for Peace initiative, which amounts to no more than an occasional joint exercise between NATO and former Warsaw Pact troops, is widely regarded as a farce. The hope that once existed that the initiative would lead to eventual integration has proved quite unfounded.

Strangely, few questions of principle are raised against the eastward expansion of NATO. Such arguments as there are tend to be technical, and are often badly flawed. It is sometimes claimed, for example, that the admission of former Communist states would lead to such diversity in NATO that its effectiveness would necessarily be diluted. Yet NATO members already range from the mighty United States to semipacifist Denmark. They include Luxembourg, whose armed forces number fewer than 1,000 men, and Iceland, which has no army at all. They include Greece and Turkey, which, but for NATO, might well have gone to war with each other on more than one occasion. A second argument, that there are logistical difficulties in the way of military integration, is likewise without much foundation. It takes no account of the structural reforms that the Visegrad countries (Czech Republic, Hungary, Poland, and Slovakia) in particular have begun precisely in order to make themselves compatible with NATO armies. It would not be significantly more difficult to integrate the armed forces of, say, Hungary or even Estonia than it was to link up those of Spain.

The real question is whether the West is wise to bow to Russian pressure against the enlargement of NATO. I do not think so. There is no question of NATO's ever having had or being likely to have aggressive intentions toward Russia. Russia's insistence on having her way in the matter must be due to her dislike of the fact that Poland, Hungary, the Czechs, and Slovakia would, if they join NATO, be under the protection of the West. This resentment is sinister. It carries with it the implication that Russia retains designs on these countries. If this is true, then it becomes a matter of urgency that they join NATO.

The failure of will in NATO is indicative of a more profound weakness in the West. On both sides of the Atlantic, NATO is increasingly seen as an irrelevance by governments eager to reap premature dividends from the end of the Cold War. Against a background of rapidly falling defense spending, there is a rise of anti-Americanism in Europe and isolationism in the United States. The economic introversion of figures like Pat Buchanan and James Goldsmith is matched by an introversion in foreign and defense policy.

The Clinton presidency has seen an unprecedented subjugation of foreign policy imperatives to domestic needs. A widespread criticism of President Bush was that he had allowed foreign policy to distract him from the home agenda, and Clinton made electoral promises to concentrate on economic and social policy. Yet even Clinton's most ardent admirers must concede that the president's determination to sacrifice foreign policy interests in the so far largely unsuccessful attempts to force through his domestic pro-gram has damaged the United States' long-term international posi-tion. Policy on both Cuba and Haiti was dictated by the need to win congressional support for domestic policies. In the case of Haiti, this took the form of a straightforward deal with the Black Caucus: the Caucus's support for the Healthcare Bill in return for a pledge to unseat Haiti's mulatto elite. The decision to award a visa to Gerry Adams before the IRA had declared a cease-fire, and the subsequent decision to recognize Sinn Féin and welcome Adams to the White House, displayed the same sense of priorities: in this case, the weakening of an important relationship with a friendly country in return for ethnic Irish congressional support for domestic policies.

All of this has gone hand in hand with the most savage defense cuts in American history. During the period of office of the present administration, the U.S. Air Force is preparing for eventual

Fig. 9.
NATO DEFENSE EXPENDITURES AS PERCENT OF GDP (a):

Country	Average 1970–1974	Average 1975–1979	Average 1980–1984	Average 1985–1989	1988	1989	1990	1991	1992	1993	1994	(b) 1995
Belgium	2.9	3.2	3.3	2.9	2.7	2.5	2.4	2.3	1.9	1.8	1.7	1.7
Denmark	2.4	2.4	2.4	2.1	2.1	2.1	2.0	2.1	2.0	2.0	1.9	1.8
France	3.9	3.8	4.1	3.8	3.8	3.7	3.6	3.6	3.4	3.4	3.3	3.1
Germany (c)	3.5	3.4	3.4	3.0	2.9	2.8	2.8	2.3	2.1	1.9	1.8	1.7
Greece	4.7	6.7	6.6	6.3	6.3	5.7	5.8	5.4	4.6	4.5	4.5	4.6
Italy	2.5	2.0	2.1	2.3	2.3	2.3	2.1	2.1	2.0	2.1	2.0	1.9
Luxembourg	0.8	1.0	1.2	1.1	1.3	1.1	1.1	1.2	1.0	0.9	0.9	0.8
Netherlands	3.1	3.1	3.1	2.9	3.0	2.8	2.6	2.5	2.5	2.3	2.2	2.1
Norway	3.3	3.1	2.9	3.2	3.2	3.3	3.2	3.1	3.4	3.1	3.1	2.9
Portugal	6.9	3.9	3.4	3.2	3.2	3.2	3.1	3.1	2.7	2.6	2.5	2.7
Spain	—	—	2.3	2.2	2.1	2.1	1.8	1.7	1.6	1.7	1.5	1.5
Turkey	3.4	4.4	4.0	3.3	2.8	3.1	3.5	3.8	3.9	3.9	4.0	3.9
United Kingdom	5.0	4.9	5.2	4.6	4.2	4.1	4.1	4.3	3.8	3.6	3.3	3.1
NATO Europe	—	—	**3.6**	**3.3**	**3.2**	**3.1**	**3.0**	**2.9**	**2.6**	**2.6**	**2.4**	**2.3**
Canada	2.1	1.9	2.1	2.1	2.1	2.0	2.0	1.9	1.9	1.9	1.8	1.6
United States	6.5	5.1	5.8	6.3	6.1	5.8	5.6	5.0	5.1	4.8	4.3	4.0
NATO Total	—	—	**4.6**	**4.7**	**4.5**	**4.4**	**4.1**	**3.7**	**3.7**	**3.6**	**3.3**	**3.0**

(a) NATO definition of defense expenditure as a proportion of gross domestic product (based on current prices)—not available.

(b) 1995 figures are estimates.

(c) These percentages have been calculated without taking into account the expenditure for Berlin.

Source: *NATO press release M-DPC-2(95)115-'Financial & Economic Data Relating to NATO Defence' Table 3.*

cuts of nearly 60 percent of its strength, and the navy of 100 ships. The Pentagon announced in 1994 that all its orders were delayed. By 1999, U.S. military spending in real dollar terms will be lower than at any time since before World War II. *The Washington Post* has calculated that the United States could no longer launch an overseas operation on the scale of Desert Storm.

Growing isolationism in the United States is more than matched by its European counterparts. The current determination in the European Union to downgrade the Atlantic Alliance, specifically by building up the Western European Union as a rival to NATO, draws on a long history of anti-Americanism in Europe.

Charles de Gaulle, whose personality dominated Western European as well as French politics during the critical early years of the European Community, made no attempt to disguise his view that Europe, under French leadership, should "counterbalance" the U.S. and Soviet blocs. Writing in his memoirs, he painted a detailed picture of the kind of European association he envisaged. It would be dominated by France, which would "play a splendid role and greatly further her own interests and those of the human race." Africa, which he saw essentially as part of a greater France, would be part of a European bloc that would take its place alongside a capitalist-American bloc in the Western hemisphere and a Soviet Communist bloc in Asia. France would sit "in a position of authority on the old continent, while America would find herself back in her hemisphere and Britain on her island."★

Large parts of the European left also adopted the dogma of anti-Americanism. Socialist intellectuals promoted the notion of moral equivalence between the superpowers. Thus, the Russian invasion of Afghanistan was depicted as being no worse than U.S.

★Charles de Gaulle, *Le Salut: 1944–46* (Plon, 1959).

intervention in Nicaragua. In the eyes of many continental Social Democrats, especially in Germany, Europe stood as a civilized bulwark against the ideological barbarism of both Eastern and Western blocs. There was a European "third way" or "special path" between the excesses of American capitalism and the totalitarianism of Russian Communism.

One of the effects of the end of the Cold War has been to breathe new life into European anti-Americanism. The European Commission's fear of "American cultural imperialism," given expression in the protectionist regulations of its Cultural Directorate DG-X, prevented a properly liberal resolution of the GATT negotiations. The dislike of American superiority in the film industry, for example, has not only led the Commission to grant huge subsidies to the European audio-visual sector, but also to propose more than 10 percent of all air-time be reserved for programs of European origin. EU policy on public procurement is openly protectionist. It requires national governments to give preference to European bids over those from "third countries" unless the "third country" bid is at least 3 percent lower than its nearest EU rival. This policy was fiercely opposed by the United Kingdom, which is the only member government regularly to open procurement to competitive tender; other governments more often simply hand contracts out after private discussions. Its chief effect has therefore been to oblige the United Kingdom to accept inferior European bids over Asian or American ones. The agricultural, coal, steel, and textile industries are heavily protected by subsidies and EU tariffs.

One of Helmut Kohl's former chief foreign policy advisers, Horst Teltschik, has actually called for a "United Europe" to step into the place of the Soviet Union as America's chief opponent and adversary, declaring: "It is a good thing for every superpower to have a rival of equal strength, keeping the scales in balance. The history of the last few decades shows that there are many on this planet who favor having a counterweight to the USA or an alternative. As a European, I say that a Europe in the process of integration should take on that role."

Much of this kind of thinking is now coloring the Union's approach to defense and security. It is difficult to deny that the EU's emphasis on an exclusively European defense identity owes more to dogma than to a practical assessment of Europe's security needs. The new Euro-Corps, for example, which brings troops from France, Germany, Belgium, Luxembourg, and Spain under a common military command, is being built up as a symbol of European unity despite the fact that it is riven by problems of language and incompatible weapons systems and is militarily almost useless. Nor are political difficulties ever far from its surface. When Belgian troops joined what had until then been a Franco-German initiative, a mighty row ensued over whether Flemish should be the third working language of the Corps. (A Belgian compromise proposal to adopt English as the common language of command was, unsurprisingly, rejected out of hand). There was another diplomatic squabble when, as part of the Bastille Day celebrations in 1994, Euro-Corps troops were required to salute President Mitterrand as their commander-in-chief. The Spanish military establishment was especially unhappy at the idea, pointing out that only the King of Spain was entitled to receive the salute, and that it was inappropriate to dip the Spanish flag (which incorporates the coat of arms of the ruling Bourbon dynasty) before "the legal and political heir of Robespierre. Such difficulties echo those of the Austro-Hungarian army, which, likewise torn by national and linguistic rivalries, was quite ineffective as a military force.

Equally misconceived is the notion that the exclusively European defense organization, the Western European Union, can be built up as an active military organization outside NATO's command structure. The WEU lacks troops and material of its own, and must therefore "borrow" from its members, who are also NATO members. Only the United States is able to provide NATO with certain key strategic components, notably air- and sea-lift fleets, reconnaissance and communications satellites, certain advanced aircraft, and various military computers. The idea that Europe can be secure without the American alliance (let alone the neo-Gaullist concept that that alliance should be replaced by open rivalry) is wrong and dangerously so.

Few are prepared to argue openly that Europe should actively seek to rid itself of the American military connection. Even the most extreme anti-Americans have the tactical sense to present their case as pure pragmatism. The Americans, they argue, are leaving Europe whether Europeans like it or not. With the end of the Cold War, the U.S. has no strategic interest in Europe and can no longer justify the expense of defending Europe's interests. Europe must therefore be prepared to fill the vacuum left by the departing troops; it must begin to look to its own defense.

This reasoning misses a critical point: NATO structures will still be in place regardless of any diminution of the American presence in Europe. Every EU state continues to be protected by the most successful military alliance in history, one whose integrated command structure will outlast a partial American troop withdrawal. There is no reason why, as the U.S. presence diminishes, Europeans should not step into posts in the NATO command vacated by Americans. It makes no sense to go to the immense trouble of building a new defense structure when one already exists that cannot easily be improved upon. Even with a diminished U.S. presence in Europe, NATO will continue to provide the guarantee of U.S. and Canadian assistance in the event of an external threat to European security, as well as the irreplaceable benefit of a structure that will involve U.S. forces in out-of-area NATO operations across the world.

The case being made against NATO is neither pragmatic nor strategic. On the Western shores of the Atlantic, it is the cry of pure isolationism: the U.S. should abandon its attempts to make the world secure. It should turn in on itself, heedless of the consequences for stability and freedom in the world it must inhabit. In Europe, the case against NATO is the authentic voice of Euronationalism. If the European Union is to become a state, it follows that it must have all the attributes and trappings of a state: a currency, a parliament, a diplomatic service, a flag, a judicial system, a supreme court, external borders, a passport, a national anthem, a president. How can this list be complete without the addition of that most fundamental symbol of statehood, a national army? Whatever the consequences in terms of diminished strength and security, Europe must have its own armed force if it is to become a true political unit.

The difficulties faced by NATO symbolize the problems the West as a whole has encountered since the fall of the Berlin Wall. What should have been a golden opportunity to spread the Western values of political and economic freedom across the world has been thrown away through simple lack of willpower. The end of the Cold War has allowed seething tensions to burst out, but the West has either failed to meet the new challenges or actually exacerbated the problems. Protectionism, anti-Atlanticism, military irresolution, the abandonment of a belief in the absolute superiority of the liberal-capitalist model: all this has followed from the end of the

Cold War and the evaporation of the faith that once sustained the West. If a new world order is to develop, it will require the formulation of an active and coherent Western agenda.

Where states with non-Western cultural backgrounds have adopted liberal-democratic systems, they should be supported positively. This is not neocolonialism. Democracy has not made Japan any less Asian or Turkey any less Levantine. These countries show that Western models can be adapted to fit Confucian-type or Islamic cultures. They represent the hope of spreading the universal values of a new world order. It is astonishing, then, that the West should be so ready to indulge in regular political outbursts against them.

Western policy toward Turkey typifies the problem. Turkey is a fierce and loyal Western ally of long standing. It was a reliable and important NATO member. It represents the best hope of demonstrating to the rest of the Islamic world that secular democracy works, that it brings concrete economic and political benefits. In the vital strategic region of Central Asia, Turkey is the only force working for stability and democracy. It is one of the three main regional powers, along with Russia, whose main contribution is to prop up ex-Communist governments in an attempt to maintain its hegemony in the region, and Iran, which is exporting a violent brand of fundamentalism to Central Asian Muslims. Against these two destabilizing and anti-Western ideologies, Turkey is arguing for its moderate brand of pro-Western secular Islam.

Freedom and stability in the world require active and constant support. Working to create a decent order in the world, based on liberal values, is as much in the narrow interest of the West as it is a moral imperative. As has so often been the case down the ages, there is a convergence between selfish and altruistic determinants of foreign policy.

Meanwhile, the prospect of a stable world has receded. While the West has squandered seven years of opportunity to consolidate the strength of its position following the "defeat" of Soviet Communism, the East has been looking on and drawing its own conclusions. The view is growing in Asia that the contest of cultures between Confucian-authoritarianism and Christian-liberalism may not now be as one-sided as had been thought. In terms of world equilibrium this matters if the resulting tension between East and West spills over into major conflict. Any further weakening of resolve in the West, especially on the central issue of free trade, will heighten this possibility.

It is therefore of the greatest importance to assess what direction thinking in the West is now taking.

CHAPTER FOUR

EUROPE: THE SUPER TRADE BLOC

A MAJOR CONTRIBUTING factor to the recent under-mining of the Western cultural tradition—and especially of the ideal of free trade—has been the development in the West of the trade bloc. In this process the nations of Europe have led the way, just as they did in the development of a liberal economic ethos. Europe currently provides the only genuinely working model of an advanced industrial trade bloc in action. Its future provides one of the keys to an assessment of where Western economic and political philosophy will end up.

Sometimes under the guise of free trade—but decreasingly so—the European Union, both by design and by legal and consti-tutional practice, is currently shaping itself into a clearly defined protected single market. As such, the European experience enables one to address a string of related questions. Does a single market, as opposed to a free trading market, necessitate the formation of a single economy, defined in particular by the establishment of a single currency? Is it possible to have a single currency without a single government? Is not the management of a single currency the essence of a single government? Will a single government managing a group of nations as varied as those of Europe be of necessity expensive and oppressive? Does that not mean high taxes and high costs to industry? Will not this require raising further barriers to trade associated with the formation of the original single market? Is there not in other words a direct link between the initial desire for a single market, whose motivation was addressed in Chapter 2, and ever-increasing centralization and protectionism?

The founding fathers of the European Common Market who really mattered were French.* French philosophy and interest dominated not only the original design but also the development of European unification from the formation of the European Coal and Steel Community at the Treaty of Paris in 1951 to the point of British entry and the rise of German influence in 1973. Interestingly, the only serious previous attempt to form a European trade bloc, some hundred and fifty years earlier, had also been French inspired. Napoleon's Continental System, which was a trading disaster and which collapsed in 1814, was built from a position of political strength. The Common Market, on the other hand, was formed from a sense of weakness by countries who at one point or another had been defeated during World War II. The Continental System and the Common Market both were founded in part to challenge what the French perceived as unacceptable Anglo-Saxon ambitions. The Treaty of Rome, signed in March 1957, which because it became binding on the citizens as well as the governments of the signatory countries was not so much a treaty as the makings

---

*For a fuller account of the formation of the European Union, see Michael Spicer, *A Treaty Too Far* (Fourth Estate, 1992).

of a new European constitution,* was formulated on the basis of two highly debatable assumptions: first, that the cause of war in Europe had been the rivalry between nation-states (ignoring the effect of a pan-European fascist movement) so that peace would be assured only if national differences were suppressed and were ultimately superseded by some form of grand federation (the founding fathers of Europe did not have the benefit of the Yugoslavian experience or of the breakup of the Soviet Union); second, that the way to compete with the Anglo-Saxon United States was by way of a large protected home market.

Each of these two ideas can be traced through every stage of the development of the European Union. For a while the larger-than-life presence of General de Gaulle gave the illusion that Europe might develop toward a loose association of sovereign nation-states. The French walkout from the Council of Ministers in 1965 and the consequent apparent acceptance through the so-called Luxembourg Compromise of the ultimate supremacy of the national interest gave some reassurance to those who were alarmed about the formation of a federal state. But the respite was an illusion, not to say a delusion.

Self-delusion has been a recurring feature of the history of the development of the European Union. The belief of the French that they could create a protectionist, interventionist single market while retaining in Paris all important aspects of sovereignty was matched by the conviction of the British that they could maintain a free market agenda while ignoring all the interventionist paraphernalia insisted on by the other member states. The Italians for their part have kidded themselves that a nonelected, nonaccountable

---

*Unlike other international treaties, the Treaty of Rome requires that its provisions, as well as any subsequent rulings made by the institutions it established, be incorporated into the national law of its signatories.

system of federal government would somehow make up for the corruption and democratic deficiencies at home. The Greeks, the Portuguese, and the Irish seem to have been blissfully unaware that there was a price to pay for the handouts from Brussels in the form of the high interest rates (and unemployment) necessary to bring their currencies into alignment with the others. The Germans will, one suspects, be the next to have their illusions shattered. They believe that they will be able to "opt out" from the single currency despite the fact that they failed to add a protocol to the Treaty of Maastricht to this effect.

Whether a stable new state can be built on a pile of illusions is another matter. The question can be put another way. Will the present self-driven rush toward the formation of a protectionist state of Europe be halted and perhaps reversed by the "natural" laws of trade and liberalism developed in the West so successfully for so many centuries?

In the end the natural order will undoubtedly reassert itself. It is not possible to hide forever from reality, and the shock of emerging once more into the open can be traumatic, as it is for a prisoner tasting freedom after a long sentence. The history of the Soviet Union gives testimony both to the ultimate futility of attempting to buck the real world and to the aftershocks of having done so.

Whatever the longer-term future, the omens for the foreseeable future are not good in Europe; there the logic of the trade bloc psychology and the capacity for self-delusion may have some way to run.

So far as logic is concerned, there is a continuum that starts with the perceived need to protect a large home market comprising a collection of countries of varying shapes and sizes. From this variety flows the perceived requirement to accumulate powers at a central point in order to make the market work properly. This leads inexorably to the call for the single market to become a single economy with its own exclusive currency. Thus does the formation of a protected trade bloc lead to the adoption of the primary feature of a single state.

The process of moving along this continuum is now firmly established within the European Union. The creation of a protected single market is certainly well advanced. In particular, ways have been found to exploit fully the loopholes to free trade conveniently provided by the GATT charter. As an example, Articles XI and XVI, which permit exemptions for agriculture, provide the justification for the appallingly protectionist and wasteful Common Agricultural Policy, currently costing every citizen of the EU 100 dollars a year in taxes, not to mention the hardship to the consumer, who pays massively inflated prices. (In Britain this was calculated in 1995 at 50 dollars per week per family of four). Even more basic to the existence of the European Union is Article XXIV of GATT, which permits members of trade blocs to cut tariffs between each other while retaining them against third countries.

It is, however, with respect to their treatment of the GATT rules on antidumping that the EU authorities have demonstrated some of their greatest creative powers. The rate at which "threatened" businesses in the Union have argued successfully in Brussels for protection against "dumped" goods (i.e., goods whose prices are considered unrealistically low) has grown rapidly in recent times; it is now running at about fifty a year. Once they have agreed to an "antidumping" measure, the usual practice is for the EU authorities to permit it to remain in place despite the fact that the exporter to the EU may have markedly raised the offending price. Antidumping measures are thus becoming less to do with retaliation against "unfair" competition and more to do with protection against competition itself.

Much the same can be said of the increasing insistence by the EU authorities on the harmonization of technical and, increasingly, environmental standards of imports with those of EU manufactures. As the German influence has grown in the European Union, so has this peculiarly German form of protectionism. Harmonization as a means of protecting home industries has indeed been perfected in Germany over many years under the watchful eye of Deutsche Industrie Norm (DIN). Even with respect to intra-EU trade, DIN approval is still required on many products, despite the fact that EU regulations state that the only approval necessary is from the country of origin.

The procedures associated with the requirement for technical compatibility and standards—even where, by any objective criteria, these may be higher in the country of origin—has grown into an art form in the European Union. The use of environmental standards is fast catching up. Now being mooted is the idea that goods imported into the EU should bear a certificate to the effect that they have been manufactured under conditions of "good labor practice." This would be capable of being applied to any product made with higher labor costs than those that were currently the norm within the EU. Leaving aside the detrimental effect on trade of protective intervention to impose standards, it can be lethal to the development of the product itself. This was clearly the case with the fatal High Definition Television standard imposed by the Commission in the 1980s, which played its part in killing off this industry altogether.

The extensive use of public monies for the support of ailing industries is another way the European Union protects its manufacturers without apparently coming into direct conflict with GATT. This takes two forms. On the one hand the Commission turns a blind eye to the granting of subsidies by governments to their industries (for instance, in 1994 the sum of 20 billion francs was granted to Air France and 2.5 billion francs to Groupe Bull); on the other hand the Commission increasingly directs its own growing budgets to "supportive" projects such as the planned 15 billion dollar budget for the cinema industry. One can only hope that this does not have the same detrimental effect on that industry as the one suffered by audio-visual software from directives restricting foreign programs on European television.

All these restrictive measures have to be seen against the backdrop of a noticeable slowing down of the pace at which Europe is moving toward an openly competitive market, which, as part of the Single European Act 1986, was meant to have been fully introduced by 1 January 1993. The European Parliament, in particular, has recently been playing an increasing role in frustrating the introduction of full competition in such industries as energy generation and telecommunications.

The anticompetitive attitude in Europe vis-à-vis the telecommunications industry is a major reason why, for instance, telecommunication costs in Germany add up to twice the proportion versus sales revenues of that in the United States and Japan. This has nothing to do with unfair competition and everything to do with the short-term, counterproductive attempt to protect; it is all about the fear in France and Germany, in particular, that their telecommunications industry may have to shed the 100,000 or so employees that British Telecom has found it necessary to jettison as a result of privatization. Much the same could be said of electricity generation, where again Britain alone in Europe has opened the windows to free competition, with dramatic effects on productivity. This writer was reprimanded when he made a speech in Florida as minister for electricity in 1988 encouraging the free flow of U.S. capital into the British generating industry once it was privatized.* (At that point it was planned to privatize the nuclear as well as the nonnuclear generating capacity; the nuclear side was thought to be politically too "hot" for it to be permitted to accept foreign investment).

This panoply of protective measures, growing rapidly at a time when GATT has been priding itself through the completion of the Uruguay Round on having extended tariff reform from manufacturing to the services sector, has gone hand in hand with a massive shift of power from national governments to the burgeoning federal one. The point to reemphasize is that the French architects of the European Union always conceived of the move from a protected trade bloc to greater central intervention as an essential and wholly logical step. In the late 1960s Jean-Jacques Servan-Schreiber put it like this: "The two conditions necessary for an efficient European organization are, first, authority in certain areas over the individual nation-states and, second, its own financial resources so that it can carry out large-scale projects."* In his next sentence, Servan-Schreiber takes the matter to its logical conclusion: "Hobbled by its rule of unanimity, the confederation encourages abstention rather than action and, to use the vocabulary of economics, free trade rather than joint policies, laissez faire rather than decisive action." The attack on free trade and the formation of a federal state are inextricably bound together. Without the one you do not have the other.

This has indeed provided a clear guide to the development of

---

*I was chided again when I suggested that British Coal should be privatized at the same time as the electricity industry.

*Jean-Jacques Servan-Schreiber, *The American Challenge* (Hamish Hamilton, 1968).

the European Union. Protectionist policies have been accompanied by measures to formalize the accumulation of power at the center. Some of these actions have required amendment to the Treaty of Rome. The principle of majority voting, defined by Servan-Schreiber as the distinguishing feature of a federal state as against a confederation, was introduced in the Single European Act, which came into force in 1986 and was further extended in 1992 by the Treaty of Maastricht.

Most of the movement toward a centralized state of Europe is now self-propelled and does not require any further amendment to the original Treaty.

The European Union operates on the basis of the *occupied field doctrine*. This holds that EU authority is irreversibly entrenched in any area where it has once legislated. It is the source of the "ratchet effect," "one-way street," and "conveyor belt" metaphors. Article B of the Maastricht Treaty pledges "to maintain in full and build on the *acquis communautaire*" (i.e., the accumulated body of established Community law), thereby giving legal recognition to this process for the first time.

Another factor leading to the automatic centralization of power lies in the motivation of the main institutions of the European Union. Both the Commission and the European Court of Justice see their role as being to bring as many fields of policy as possible into the EU's administrative domain. As long ago as 1970 the Commission was defined, by Franco Malfatti, president of the European Commission, as "at one and the same time the guardian of the Treaties and the motive force for integration." The Commission is not only given the authority to hasten moves to integration but defines its success in terms of so doing. Emile Noël, a former secretary general of the Commission, writing in an official EC publication in 1988, explained its powers clearly. "Everything to do with economic union was left blank in the Treaty, but blanks can be filled by the institutions. There is no need for fresh treaties or fresh parliamentary ratification."

The European Court of Justice takes the same line, but with even more serious consequences. Like the Commission, it defines its success in terms of promoting integration. In the *Netherlands* versus *High Authority* case of 1960, the power of the Court to rule in complaints against member states was described as "the *ultima ratio* enabling the Community interests enshrined in the Treaty to prevail over the inertia and resistance of the Member States." The Court's judgments are final and binding; there is no appeal beyond them. Its methods are therefore crucially important. There is now an almost complete consensus among lawyers across Europe that the European Court has ceased simply to perform an interpretive or judicial function and has adopted a policy-making or legislative role. There are several cases where the Court's judgments have undeniably ignored the law as written to favor the law *as the European Court would like it to be written*. The cases of *Costa* versus *ENEL* (1964), *Van Duyn* versus *Home Office* (1974), and *Defrenne* versus *Sabena* (1976) are among the many clear examples of the European Court's going well beyond the written text to make policy on its own. In the case of *Defrenne* versus *Sabena*, the European Court decided, on the basis of rhetoric about equality in the Treaty of Rome, to force all member states to pay men and women equally. What is significant is that the judgment was to have force only from that moment onward. It was clearly a *legislative* rather than a judicial act. Later, in the case of *Barber* versus *Guardian Royal Exchange* (1990), the European Court extended its definition of equal pay to cover a wide range of perks and pension rights; once again, the new definition was to be applicable only from that moment on.

A common tactic of the Court is to allow a member country to make some judgments for itself but, in return for this "concession," to assert its right to have made that decision had it wanted to. Thus, for example, British Sunday trading laws were left to the British government to decide in accordance with "national socio-cultural characteristics"; but the principle that the EU may alter these laws in the future was conceded in perpetuity. Commenting on the case brought by Gerry Adams, leader of Sinn Féin/IRA, against his exclusion from mainland Britain under the Prevention of Terrorism Act, Professor Hartley of the London School of Economics summarized the legal realities like this:

Judging by past performance, the European Court of Justice will probably allow the government to keep Adams out. But it may take the opportunity to lay down yet another restriction on its power to control immigration into the UK.

Even where the judgments of British courts are upheld, often the detail of the European rulings adds an additional factor to determine the future shape of how decisions are made in our national courts. Slowly and steadily European law continues to encroach.

Behind all this lies the issue of the supremacy of EU law over the legal systems of the member states. The Treaty of Rome differs from other international treaties in that it requires its provisions, as well as the regulations of the institutions established under it, to be incorporated as part of the internal laws of its member states. EU legislation is thus directly binding on people and businesses within the member states. National courts are required to give precedence to EU law over national law—even if the national legislation is adopted subsequently to the EU legislation. Since the United Kingdom's accession to the Community in 1972, all

Acts of Parliament that are deemed inadvertently to contradict Community law have been modified so as to comply with the European Communities Act. The question of whether an Act of Parliament might deliberately override Community law was for a long time a matter for debate. In the *R.V. Factortame* case of 1991, however, the European Court ruled that British courts had been right to suspend the 1988 Merchant Shipping Act, which had sought to end the practice whereby Spanish fishermen registered themselves as British in order to fish the UK fishing quota. The legal implications of this judgment are extremely significant. The precedent has now been established that European Union law is invulnerable to deliberate Acts of Parliament, and that British courts are obliged to disapply those Acts when they conflict with EU law. A growing body of legal opinion now holds that Britain is in a new legal order. According to this opinion, the 1972 Act of Accession has effectively supplanted the previous doctrine of the supremacy of Parliament, and the EU treaties have become the ultimate source of sovereignty. This view strengthens with each new Commission directive and Court ruling.

On 12 September 1993, the German supreme court at Karlsruhe made an extremely significant judgment on the compatibility of the Maastricht Treaty with the German constitution. Maastricht was valid, it ruled, but went on in effect to lay down future conditions for European integration. Such integration would be compatible with German Basic Law only if, for example, it was accompanied by an increase in "democratic legitimation" (i.e., more powers to the European Parliament).

The right of a national supreme court to make such rulings is not certain. What would be the legal position if the Karlsruhe court were to rule that some future treaty failed to meet its conditions? Would Germany be allowed a derogation from the new treaty? Would it be overruled by the European Court of Justice at Luxembourg? Or would it have to leave the European Union? The matter may come to a head shortly if the convergence conditions for European monetary union are altered (as is permissible by qualified majority). The German Bundestag has made its acceptance of a single European currency conditional on the full application of the convergence conditions.

If it has its own way, the European Court would be almost bound to determine that since no German opt-out from the currency had been attached by protocol to the Treaty of Rome (something the British have achieved), Germany has "irrevocably" lost the right to surrender sovereignty over its money. Some lawyers—notably in Germany—argue that "force majeur" will still obtain; that, as Germany is so powerful in Europe, it will "persuade" the Court—very much a political court—to do a deal so as to fudge the issue of German compliance, perhaps by ruling that there has been inadequate compliance with the convergence conditions. Such an event would call into question the very legitimacy of the law itself. It will be an acknowledgment that there are rival, potentially conflicting legal systems. If one is accustomed to believe that acceptance and compliance with a single legal authority is the very essence of a stable, free society, this prospect of future legal chaos must fill one with a deep dread.

The question has arisen whether or not the process is irrevocable. Is it the case that national parliaments have merely lent their sovereign rights to the federal bodies and that, should they wish to do so, they can repeal the relevant national legislation unilaterally? Or is it the case that even in this matter of revocation, the Treaty of Rome now binds member states to each other; that for a country to leave the system would require an appropriate amendment, not to national legislation but to the treaty itself, and that this would require the unanimous approval of the other members? In this case, it would be impossible for members to leave the Union of their own free will. The only precedent is that of Greenland, which left the EU in 1984 (thereby halving its land surface). Greenland's secession was agreed to by all the other member states; the question of what would happen if one country's withdrawal were opposed by the others has not yet arisen.

Most British constitutional lawyers I have talked to maintain the position that as a matter of Realpolitik, if not of law, the British Parliament could still repeal the Treaty of Accession of 1972. They say, however, that it would be wise to amend the Treaty of Rome specifically to accommodate this if there were any thought that the option would be needed.

If there is an element of uncertainty about the present ability of national parliaments successfully to challenge the rulings of the European Court, if necessary by threatening to revoke the national legislation that provided it with its original powers, there can be no such doubt about the "irrevocable" nature of the main ingredient of the Treaty of Maastricht. Unless the main terms of this treaty, initialed by heads of governments on 10 December 1991, are revoked, the days of the sovereign nation-state in Europe are numbered. What was so distinctive about the Treaty of Maastricht was that for the first time in the history of the European Union, the concept of "irrevocability" was built into the Treaty of Rome. Its signatories agreed to a timetable for the introduction of an "irrevocable" single currency. This word "irrevocable" (Paragraph 4, Article 109 [1] of the Treaty of Maastricht) is of profound significance, nowhere more so than in the United Kingdom, whose unwritten constitution virtually hangs on the notion that no one parliament may bind another and that therefore each individual parliament is sovereign.

Almost as significant as the inclusion of the word "irrevocable" was the fact that Maastricht fixed a specific date by which a single currency had to be introduced. Paragraph 4 of Article 109j reads: "If by the end of 1997 the date for the beginning of the third stage [defined in the treaty as involving the establishment of a single currency] has not been set, the third stage shall start on 1 January 1999."

There are no "ifs" or "buts" about this. It is true that Britain and Denmark have signed protocols to the treaty permitting them to opt-out of these arrangements; but it has been the long-held view of people like myself who opposed the ratification of the Treaty of Maastricht by the British Parliament that the formation of a single currency was a matter so profound that no country would be able to sustain for long the position of being a member of the European Union, as presently constituted, while at the same time remaining outside its monetary system. The probability was that both Britain and Denmark would in the end have no choice but to join a single currency once it was established. Particularly unrealistic was the German view that having fully signed up to the concept and to the introductory date of the single currency, conditions attached to joining by the Bundestag would have any force of law.

Maastricht has cleared the decks for the formation of a single state of Europe. Unless the Treaty of Rome is further amended, a single currency will be established inevitably, irrevocably, and as a matter of law. When it is operational, the nation-state in Europe will have ceased to exist. A country that is no longer responsible for its own money is no longer an independent nation.

The process from protectionism to federalism will have been completed, as was the logical intention of the founding fathers.

The question central to this book is not so much whether this will be good or bad for the people of Europe but what it will do for the future of world trade.

I have already argued that the European Union was born from a strong desire to protect its industries and that it has made extensive use of the appropriate instruments for achieving this. The first question concerns the extent to which the EU has been successful in achieving its protectionist aims and the second is whether, having formed itself into a federal state, the European Union will change its spots and return to the past liberal traditions of many of its constituent members.

EU protectionism has been particularly effective with respect to trade with the former Soviet satellite countries on its eastern borders. The EU has imposed tariffs on the Central and Eastern European countries that effectively surpass anything seen during the Cold War. The emerging democracies, desperately seeking economic and political stability, have found that the free market reforms urged on them by the EU have led directly to Brussels' taking action to close markets to their goods. Hungary, for example, is now allowed to export less than 6,397.6 tons of beef per year to the EU before 1997, as compared to some 98,425.2 tons per year sold in the mid 1970s to a smaller Community. There now exists the unedifying spectacle of the European Union lecturing its neighbors on the merits of free markets while it dumps its artificially created surplus agricultural products on them and effectively shuts the door to their produce. In 1993 the EU even had to resort to a scare over foot and mouth disease to ban all beef from Poland—ignoring the fact that foot and mouth disease had been unknown in Poland for eighteen years, whereas it continued to be prevalent in Portugal and elsewhere within the EU.

Similar tactics are used by the Union against their vulnerable neighbors with respect to textiles and steel. The antidumping technique has been used to particular effect against Czech steel.

There is no doubting the nature of the past pattern of EU trade policy; the question is whether it will change in the future. The omens are that it will get worse—that is, become increasingly restrictive. There is a spiraling process that affects all protected economies and will be compounded by the very nature of the European Union. Industries that are protected from the spur of competition tend to become more inefficient and even less capable of competing against the outside; the cry of "unfair competition" becomes even more shrill, and the pressure accumulates for even greater protection.

In the case of the emerging European federal state, there exist special circumstances that will aggravate this process. In particular, common standards of employment will require elaborate arrangements for their enforcement, together with expensive payments to those former countries that cannot keep up. This, in turn, will mean the imposition of new taxes, which will fall mainly on the shoulders of the taxpayers of the richer former countries; this in turn will force up further the already high tax and social cost burdens on industry in the relatively efficient parts of Europe.

The most damaging effect from the point of view of Europe's competitiveness will come about through the introduction of the single currency. To start with, massive further transfer payments will be required from the efficient areas to make up for the devastating "social" effects in the poor areas of having to sustain price levies set in the rich countries. (Greek wage packets, for example, will be expected to buy goods at German prices.) In

1974 the Commission's own study, the MacDougal Report, estimated that these transfer costs would amount to 56 billion pounds
per year for Britain alone. These "cohesion" funds will further
drain the efficient economies. Gradually, perhaps not so gradually,
all areas will be reduced in wealth and cost efficiency toward the
lowest common denominator. In these circumstances, the idea
that the protectionist philosophy, which was itself the driving
force behind the creation of the trade bloc, will abate is hardly
realistic; far more probable is that the protectionist pressures will
harden.

This probability will become a virtual certainty when account
is taken of the fact that with a single currency European countries
will have all but cut themselves off from the alternative to more
protection as the response to cheap imports. The free marketeer's
response to chronic uncompetitiveness is not to restrict trade but
to allow prices to readjust; in the context of international trade
this requires freely floating exchange rates. Leaving aside any
philosophical objections to this within the European Union, it is
likely to be much harder with a single currency to achieve conditions where prices of EU goods on the world market truly reflect
their costs. The aggregation involved with a single currency will
mean loss of flexibility for individual countries. Poorer nations
will be particularly hard hit because the value of their currency
will largely reflect productivity and cost structures in the powerful
economies of Europe. Portuguese unit costs, for instance, much
less powerful in determining the value of the single currency than,
say, German unit costs, will be "lost in the noise." Portuguese
costs relative to Japanese costs will not be reflected in the rate of
exchange between Portugal and Japan. The relative prices of Japan
and Portugal will therefore be out of line, to the detriment of
trade between them. The exchange value of Japanese goods against

German goods will also be distorted because Germany will have to an extent been aggregated to the level of Portugal. In other words Germany will be paying too high a price than is economically necessary for her imports.

The single currency will be too blunt an instrument for determining the exchange values of aggregated but still very different economies against those of outside countries. For this reason the floating exchange option as a means of adjusting relative competitiveness will in effect be denied to a federal state of Europe. In the event of a serious imbalance of trade arising with non-EU countries, further protectionism will be the only recourse open to the Union.

For Europeans, as I argue further in Chapter 6, this is a serious matter. Protectionism slows down the economic advance of producers and consumers alike. The question, central to this book, is what will be the effect of a "fortress Europe" policy on the rest of the world?

The present signs are that rising protectionism in Europe will have little or no effect on the countries of the Far East. They seem set to forge ahead regardless of neither the economic performance of European countries nor the philosophies by which they manage themselves. In particular, they appear to be totally impervious to European notions of limiting world trade. Certainly there has been great resistance among the seventeen countries that make up the Asia–Pacific Economic Cooperation (APEC) against any moves to turn themselves into anything other than a free trade zone. The leaders of the Association of South East Asian Nations (ASEAN) specifically declared in 1994 that "ASEAN, unlike the European Community, will remain an association of sovereign states." The appreciation appears to be widespread throughout the countries of the Orient that it is the free trading experience—and that alone—that is serving them so well.

Not quite the same mood prevails in the Americas. Here the European call for centrally coordinated protectionism is beginning to find its echo, so much so that it merits closer inspection.

CHAPTER FIVE

NAFTA AND
THE AMERICAS

MORE SO THAN in Europe, the response in the Americas to what is seen as unfair competition from the East is couched in the language of free trade. Very few commentators in North America, at least, talk of NAFTA in terms of its protectionist potential. The very name—North American Free Trade Area—would suggest the exact opposite. The Perotists and the Buchananists have argued indeed that it is a shameless destruction of the required safeguards for the domestic U.S. market.

It is true also that NAFTA has neither the constitutional nor the philosophical impetus of the European Union toward becoming a full-blooded protectionist trade bloc. Its central aim remains the abolition of barriers to trade and investment. There are, however, signs that the organization may be moving in a direction not wholly foreseen by its founders. As in Europe, a central issue concerns the question of the treatment of the currency exchange rates between the member countries. It was certainly conceived from the inception of NAFTA that both the Canadian dollar and the Mexican peso would need to be firmly attached, if not fixed, to the U.S. dollar. From the point of view of U.S. business, this was thought of as providing some stability for the value of U.S. investments—in particular those made in Mexico—to compensate for low-labor-cost Mexican imports threatening U.S. domestic operations.

The run on the peso that began toward the end of 1994 was a serious matter in this context. The reaction to it was the almost universal call, especially in the United States, for tighter management of the currency relationship. This has prompted vastly expensive protective proposals comprising eventually a 54 billion-dollar (U.S.) loan guarantee scheme to support the peso. The process of moving from the abolition of barriers to trade to the cooperative and centralized management of unlike economies has begun. The early impact of such a move on the rest of the world is already becoming apparent. The anchor currency of the bloc, the U.S. dollar, has gone into what looks at times like secular decline. Despite the boost that this will give to U.S. exports, it has prompted ever louder calls for "protection," especially within the United States. Under the NAFTA agreement a new protectionist fence would need to encompass Mexico and Canada as well as the United States; a process that had started out, honorably with respect to most of its original protagonists, as a move toward freer trade would have turned into a major step in the opposite direction.

One factor modifying protectionist tendencies within NAFTA is that other trading arrangements are springing up throughout the Americas. There remains a chance that these will link together as part of a genuine process of freeing trade within a large geographical area and on a model comparable to that of APEC. Every bit as important, there is evidence of a new and healthy interplay between freer movements of trade among the countries of South America and domestic policies more closely related to market forces; most significantly, the combination of these economic forces is underpinning the reemergence of democracy through the Americas.

It is certainly the case that during the 1980s, significant political changes began to take place in Central and South America. In country after country, authoritarian regimes were toppled and replaced by civilian governments subscribing to democratic values.

In 1979, the Peruvian army handed power back to Fernando Belaúnde Terry, who had been overthrown by a military coup in 1968. Ecuador followed almost immediately. The oil boom there in the 1970s had created a large new middle class and to some degree removed the causes of the instability that first led to the overthrow of democracy. Uruguay was next, its generals moving aside in 1980. In 1982, defeat in the Falklands war caused a wave of popular resentment against the military regime in Argentina; the junta was forced to step down, and free elections were held. In 1985, the Brazilian military regime withdrew and allowed a transition to democracy. In the same year, elections were held in El Salvador and Guatemala. In 1989, two of the most established military supremos in South America fell from power: Chile's General Pinochet and Paraguay's General Stroessner. At the same time, the United States intervened to force Panama's Manuel Noriega from office and arrest him on drug charges. The following year, the brutal Sandinista tyranny in Nicaragua was defeated and a democratic center-right government was formed under Violeta Chamorro. Only Fidel Castro continues to hold out against the democratic tide. The area's first modern dictator has turned out to be its last.

Unsurprisingly, not every Latin American country has yet a fully matured and accountable democratic system. In Mexico, the Institutional Revolutionary Party (PRI) has held power for over seventy years during which, though broadly popular, it has resorted to occasional bribery and vote rigging. In Peru in 1992, President Alberto Fujimori dissolved the parliament and suspended the constitution; he did, however, have this action narrowly endorsed in a referendum, and was reelected with a comfortable majority in April 1995. There are still a few surviving Communist rebel groups, many of whom have set aside the rhetoric of the Cold War and instead taken up the cause of the poor indigenous peoples. Yet one should not understate the magnitude of what has happened in Latin America. In effect, the nations of Central and South America have rejoined the West.

They have returned to the political tradition in whose name they were founded. Like revolutionary France and the United States, the nations of Latin America were built by democratic idealists who saw independence as a way to usher in a new era of liberty and enlightenment. The constitutional model championed by Simón Bolívar, the Liberator, was as modern and rational as the early-nineteenth-century mind could conceive: universal male suffrage, a bill of rights, the division of powers, an independent judiciary, and so on. It was because of their liberal credentials that the newly independent American states won the strong support of Britain and the United States. George Canning, Britain's foreign secretary, ordered the British navy to support the new nations, making impossible a Spanish reconquest. U.S. president James Monroe took a similar line, declaring the Spanish-American countries to be under the special protection of the United States.

Bolívar's dream of a united Spanish-speaking federation came to nothing as local rivalries began among the liberated states. Within a few years, military leaders were seizing power in the classic Latin tradition. Bolívar died in despair a decade after the revolutions, his hopes shattered. Latin America was at this time no less politically developed than contemporary Europe, where the reactionary governments restored in 1815 brutally repressed any challenge to their narrow oligarchical rule. Latin America's political and cultural development throughout the nineteenth and twentieth centuries was entirely within the Western tradition. The obvious linguistic and cultural ties with Spain and Portugal were bolstered by massive European trade and investment. Britain, for example, invested more in Argentina during the nineteenth century than anywhere else outside the Dominions. Latin America accounted for more than 10 percent of Britain's trade between 1865 and World War I; over the same period, British holdings in the continent rose from 81 million pounds to 1.18 billion pounds. On the eve of war, Latin America accounted for an astonishing 25 percent of all British publicly issued assets. Recent studies have shown that British investment is returning to these pre-1914 patterns.

There was continuous flow of immigration from all over Europe to the region: not only Spaniards and Portuguese, but Italians, Germans, Scots, Slavs, Greeks, and Welsh were drawn to the opportunity of work in the agricultural, textile, and later, engineering sectors. These ties of blood and history affect policy to this day. José Maria Aznar, leader of the Spanish Popular Party, recently called for his country to place far more emphasis on its transatlantic links, made so strong by the two-way flow of population. In my view, Mr. Aznar's call should be vigorously supported and within the interest of a wider NATO. I return to this point in the final chapter.

More than 160 years after his death, Bolívar's dream of liberal democracy in Latin America is being realized. The civilian governments that came to power during the 1980s have, almost without exception, pursued radical privatization programs. Latin American observers blamed their poor economic performance during the 1970s and early 1980s not only on the domestic adjustments required by debt service problems, but also on failed import substitution policies. The intellectual case for protectionism was widely discredited. Individual liberty and economic freedom are now once again seen as necessary to support a healthy polity. Reflecting the new mood, a network of free trade pacts is spreading across the continent.

Among the most important of these is Mercosur, a free trade area made up of Paraguay, Brazil, Uruguay, and Argentina. From March 1991, Mercosur began an ambitious program of tariff reduction, which culminated on 1 January 1995 with the elimination of all internal tariffs. Trade between the Mercosur states increased in volume by over 100 percent over this period, and the pact has become the cornerstone of the economic policies of its members.

Between NAFTA and Mercosur, a growing web of free trade agreements threads its way across Latin America. Bolivia is an associate member of Mercosur, and aims to become a full member. It is also a member of the Andean Pact, along with Peru, Ecuador, Colombia, and Venezuela. While not as developed as Mercosur, the Andean Pact has made substantial progress toward creating a free internal market. It has a total GDP of over 130 billion dollars, and trade among its members has increased by around 25 percent a year since 1992 (despite Peru's suspension of its membership between August 1992 and April 1994). In June 1994, two of the Andean Pact countries, Colombia and Venezuela, formed a free trade area with Mexico known as the Group of Three. As well as being a member of NAFTA, Mexico has signed bilateral free trade treaties with a number of Central American states. In September 1994, it signed a free trade treaty with Chile, per capita the wealthiest and most developed country in South America, and considered a strong candidate for NAFTA membership. Chile is also an associate member of Mercosur (which it has so far refused to join fully only because it considers NAFTA membership a more important priority), thus completing the circle.

At the same time, the six-member Central American Common Market, which had broken down in the 1970s, has been resuscitated and has made considerable progress toward the liberalization of internal trade, especially in agricultural products; it is linked by free trade agreements to Mexico and Venezuela. There has also been renewed interest in the twelve-member Caribbean Common Market, which Venezuela has also joined. Finally, and of great potential importance, most of the Latin American countries are members of the Latin American Integration Association (ALADI), which requires that any benefits obtained by one of its signatories in bilateral negotiations be extended to all member states. Thus, in theory, the benefits enjoyed by Mexico as a member of NAFTA should automatically extend to every Latin American country. ALADI has no enforcement mechanism, although it does provide a forum through which NAFTA may eventually be extended southward.

The hope is that this web of bilateral and multilateral agreements will in time be drawn together into a massive free internal market. Among the strongest promoters of the various accords have been the smaller states, who are determined to maintain their access to the markets of their larger neighbors, especially the United States. It has to be accepted that part of their determination is reactive, driven by a fear that the world may break down into regional trade blocs, thereby excluding them from other developed markets. Their governments feel that they must secure the U.S. market before the erection of any U.S. tariff barriers against third countries. The United States for its part appears to be prepared to open its home market to its southern neighbors over time.

Disturbingly, the U.S. is at least partly motivated by a view that the world will coalesce into trade blocs. Much of U.S. policy remains tied to the view that the world economy is centered on that of the three major developed regions: Japan, the European Union, and the United States itself. A recurring theme of this book is that this picture of the world has been quite outdated since the late 1980s. The countries of the East, in particular, have emerged as areas of massive growth, not by "piggybacking" the developed economies, but because of their own domestic reforms. The recession of the early 1990s, described at the time as a world recession, was in fact a European recession (matched to some degree in Japan and the United States): world output continued to rise—largely on the back of the Eastern miracle.

The formation of NAFTA, and perhaps its eventual growth into a continental economic area—AFTA—need not be a further step toward a world of competing blocs. What is clear is that the development of customs unions in the Americas has reached a critical point. It is possible that the lowering of tariffs there will be a step toward freer world trade, but there is an undeniable risk that it could lead to competing European and American blocs. Let me now examine in some more detail the arguments relating to these two alternative outcomes.

CHAPTER SIX

THE TRADE PATH
TO WORLD PEACE

THE RISE OF protectionism in the West as a response to the challenge from the East is not only worrying from the point of view of world stability, it is also based on false theory and a wrongful analysis of the facts. The question—especially the political question—boils down to whether the mechanism of free trade will wipe out Western industry and thus the jobs and the prosperity that go with it. It is not only the likes of Ross Perot, Pat Buchanan, and Jimmy Goldsmith who think that it will. Maurice Allais, the French Nobel Prize winner for Economics, has published a series of articles in *Le Figaro* claiming that free trade with the East will lead to mass unemployment in the West. The British economist Adrian Wood, for his part, has focused the issue on unskilled workers. Wood argues that trade with the East diminished the demand for unskilled workers in Europe and North America by no less than 20 percent in the thirty years to 1990, with three-quarters of this decline taking place in the 1980s.

Certainly traditional economic theory would suggest that the comparative advantage of economies with relatively low productivity (output per man) lies in their cheap unskilled labor (currently 50 cents per hour in China against 25 dollars per hour in Germany). Competition from the East will be at its strongest in producing goods that require unskilled labor, with its most penetrating effect on Western markets. Goldsmith will say, Ah, but that is to miss my point. You're talking about the old world order. We could live and trade happily in that. I'm telling you the world has changed. The distinction between skilled and unskilled workers is no longer the appropriate one. What we in the West now face is the combination of very cheap workers in the East operating robot technology. This transforms them with the wave of a scientist's wand and the flick of a financier's fax machine into highly skilled workers.

Part of the answer to this lies in traditional and well-tested trade economics. This says that even if one country can produce everything more efficiently and cheaply than another, it will still pay it to specialize in those activities it does particularly well and to import those goods it produces less efficiently. The notion of "opportunity costs" in trade is as applicable today as it was when the economist and philosopher David Ricardo first expressed it at the turn of the eighteenth century. Common sense leads one to conclude that there is a cost associated with not specializing in doing those things in which one excels and of using the earnings so generated to buy in the rest.

The modern case for free trade does not rest, however, exclusively on the back of established economic theory. Its practical and visible advantages are easily demonstrated, especially in the context of the economic renaissance of the East: a resurgence itself based not on the notion of protectionist trade blocs—the APEC members have specifically turned their backs on this idea—but of free trade.

First there is the obvious point that a resurgent Asia is not only a growing competitor of the West. It is also becoming its most important customer. Asia is growing so fast as a marketplace that it is hard to keep track of its development. More than 2 billion people, a third of the world's population, have suddenly entered the global shopping mall. Millions of businesses in the West are already benefiting from this. From 1990 to 1993 the developing countries (most of whom are in the East) increased their imports by 37 percent; during the same period exports from the APEC countries rose by only 22 percent. America's exports to the latter grew by an annual average of 12 percent, while her exports to other Western countries grew by an annual average of 2 percent. The economic rise of the East was a major factor in rescuing the West from its harsh recession at the beginning of the 1990s. A policy of trade restriction would have prevented this.

None of this is to deny the strength of the competition rising in the East. The question is whether the pressure will turn out to be good or bad for the living standards of people in the West. There will undoubtedly need to be adjustments; some of them will be disruptive to the lives of many individuals. The West will find it hard to compete in the making of products that require low skills and a high intensity of labor. Western people who work in these industries will find the going tough—perhaps too tough. On the other hand, well-managed Western businesses that require high levels of skills making advanced machinery and information systems or providing commercial and financial services will see their businesses boom under conditions of free trade.

The fundamental question remains as to whether the new ease with which capital and finance flow around the world means that the West will lose its edge even in the advanced industries against what has been portrayed as a lethal combination of capital and cheap labor in the East. In a recent article, Klaus Schwab, the president of the World Economic Forum, has argued that capital today seeks out the cheapest sources of labor (*Harvard Business Review*, Nov. 1994). If this were true it would certainly suggest that the cards were now stacked against the West. But is it true?

To date, certainly, the flow of capital from West to East has not been especially high. Paul Krugman has calculated that the process has reduced Western capital stock since 1970 by 0.5 percent below what it would otherwise have been (*Harvard Business Review*, July-Aug. 1994). What is more, the investment has continued largely in the direction of extractive industries.

The fact is that Western financiers prefer on the whole to invest in the West. This is partly due to a desire to avoid taking risks in areas with which they are unfamiliar—and where, for instance, contracts do not have the backing of independent law—but it is also because (to return to Klaus Schwab's argument) labor costs have fallen dramatically in recent years as a proportion of total costs of production—in most manufacturing industries to between 5 and 10 percent of the total. The truth is that despite all the rhetoric, the root cause of the West's fear of the East—cheap labor—is not the demon it is cracked up to be. On the other hand, new demands by customers running sophisticated stock control systems for just-in-time delivery is making it more important for manufacturers to be close to their market. While this will itself undoubtedly mean more Western suppliers building their own factories in Asian countries, it will in turn provide export opportunities for Western makers of plant and machinery.

Certainly some Western businesses will find the going tough, and in many sectors there will be a growth of cheap imports, to the benefit of customers and also of manufacturers looking for cheaper raw materials and components. What is manifestly not the case is that the West faces an intrinsically impossible task in its trade relationships with the East.

Let me, however, for one moment assume that everything I have said so far is wrong: that the Ricardian laws of comparative advantage for some reason no longer apply, that because of its general sluggishness, costly working practices, defeatism, overinflated demands for standards of living that have not been earned, the West is totally inadequate on all fronts to meet the challenge from the East. In other words, let us assume that it is economically and comprehensively and across the board in danger of being wiped out. What would happen then in a free trading world? The answer is that another set of market forces would come to the rescue.

Let us assume that legislators in the United States and in the European Union are crazy enough to continue to place growing restrictions and financial burdens through various forms of taxation and bureaucratic edicts on all forms of economic activity, so that even though labor and other costs are rising in Asia (as they are), a deep and continuing imbalance of trade begins to emerge between East and West. What will be the effect of this?

A growing surplus of foreign reserves will begin to amass in Eastern coffers. This will prompt one or both of two reactions. On the one hand, there would be a massive corresponding return of the surplus to the West in the form of reverse capital flows. Beyond a certain point there will be no point in the Eastern countries' simply piling up the foreign reserves in their banks; to do so would potentially be highly inflationary for them.

These capital flows would take many forms; in part they would be purely financial: the stability of the U.S. bond market at the time of writing depends in large measure on the support it receives from Japanese sources. In part the capital flows would take the form of physical investment in plant and machinery.

Just as Japan has done in recent years, other Eastern countries would begin to invest in new ventures in the West, unless Western countries were individually or collectively mad enough to make this difficult for them by placing restrictions on foreign investment or in obstructing investors from repatriating their profits. As with Japanese investment, for instance in the British automobile industry, with the capital may come new and highly beneficial management practices that themselves set a new pace for reducing industrial costs and enabling Western companies not only to provide a better service at home but also to compete with the East.

The second effect of a shift of currency from West to East, in the absence of fixed or inflexible exchange rates, will be over time to reduce the value of Western currencies against those of the East. Western currencies will devalue until a new equilibrium point is reached where the prices of Western goods are once again competitive with those of the East.

So the best response to the type of trade imbalance feared by many people in the West is not to shut out the goods from the East and thus to deprive consumers of the additional choices they provide but to ensure that there exists a responsive exchange rate mechanism.

Three main arguments have been raised against such an arrangement, most recently by Judith Shelton in her book *Money Meltdown*. Ms. Shelton's points are important from the point of view of my arguments because they are all presented from the perspective of furthering the interests of free trade. Ms. Shelton states, first, that a floating currency encourages speculation and the nonproductive movement of funds; second, that it encourages governments, especially the powerful ones, to manipulate their own currencies in the selfish interests of their own economies. She goes so far as to say that "monetary manipulation is the most insidious form of protection." Thirdly, and most profoundly, she argues that only with a fixed system of exchange rates linked to gold will it be possible to measure the real comparative costs and efficiencies between economies. To float is to distort and to blur market signals.

Clearly it is correct that, assuming you could be sure that you had in some way fixed the "right" parity at which each of the world's currencies became irretrievably attached to an unchangeable price for gold (no mean assumption), this would impose a rigid discipline on governments to maintain anti-inflationary policies. The fact that any money they issued would have to be backed by a fixed quantity of gold would itself prevent profligate monetary and fiscal policy. The fact that they could not devalue their way out of trouble would be an added motivation toward running a sound, price-competitive economy. What is more, transaction prices between countries would reflect real cost differences unblurred by changes in the exchange rates.

There is very little that I personally can find fault with in Ms. Shelton's theoretical analysis, though I am troubled by precisely how she will determine the correct rate for each currency to link itself to gold. The problems, as far as I am concerned, are mainly practical and have to do with the real world. Judith Shelton acknowledges this herself when she asks with a note of irony: "What is the obstacle preventing a move to a global gold standard? In a word: politicians." It was the same problem recognized by John Maynard Keynes and Harry Dexter White in 1945 at Bretton Woods.

In defense of politicians, and acknowledging that I write as one, they are not perverse aberrations from the natural order. In a democracy at least they do no more and no less than reflect the basic and baser desires, the double standards, the herd instinct, the schizophrenia, the selfishness, and the desire to avoid making choices that explain much of collective human will. Societies sometimes require genuine leadership; more generally, they require an escape valve. Put another way, politicians resist arrangements that may result in mass unemployment and deprivation, however worthy the wished-for effect of ultra-sound money, because in their judgment there is only so much that their public will take.

Professor Milton Friedman—in whom there is no greater champion of sound money—recently put the same point like this:*

Today when governments in most major countries spend half or even more of the national income and exercise far greater control of the economy, no government would be willing or indeed able to submit itself to the discipline of the strict gold standard. The unwillingness of fairly closely linked countries to submit themselves to the less far-reaching discipline of the European Monetary System is surely persuasive evidence of that proposition. In today's world, political unification must precede monetary unification, not the other way round.

Nor, he feels, would things be much different if an "independent" central bank ran the economy. "It is inconceivable that a national central bank would stand idly by while changes affecting its balance of payments produced either a significant inflation or a serious recession."

The truth, perhaps the sad truth, is that a rigidly fixed system of exchange rates linked to gold or, as Professor Alan Walters (Lady Thatcher's former economic advisor) has proposed, to a fixed basket of commodities, is impractical. Governments must be left with some discretion over their financial and economic policies, if only because the circumstances may vary over time and between countries. For instance, a policy of high interest

---

*Milton Friedman, "Free Floating Anxiety" (*National Review*, Sept. 12 1994).

rates and tight money may in certain contexts be precisely the right one to dampen inflationary pressures due to excess demand. In other circumstances, where inflationary pressures are mainly due to low productivity, the one thing that may be required is to cheapen the cost of capital by reducing interest rates. This is usually the case where inflation lingers on deep into a recessionary period. In this case a tight monetary policy will indeed squeeze out the last drop of inflation, but the price of very high unemployment may be unbearable. British economic policy was coming close to this before sterling was withdrawn from the European Exchange Rate Mechanism (ERM) in September 1992. I tried to address the general point in a letter to the *London Daily Telegraph* on 8 January 1991:

Sir, your editorial (7 January) argues that a realignment of sterling within the ERM would necessarily be inflationary. Not true.

The question is, if the pound fell in value against the Deutschmark, would we spend more on more expensive foreign goods? The answer depends on the level of our purchasing power and on what economists call elasticities of demand. In the present recession a fall in the value of the pound would not mean a rise in expenditures abroad. It would probably result in a switch to cheaper British goods. It would therefore be anti-inflationary.

Furthermore, if a fall in the pound coincided with a fall in interest rates, leading to a rise in investment and productivity to match current wage demands, this too would be anti-inflationary. Low interest rates are inflationary only when they coincide with an over-heating economy as they did in 1987–8.

The more fundamental point about exchange rates is that they should not be maintained at artificial levels as is certainly the case at present, when sterling has to be supported by 14 percent interest rates.

Of course you are absolutely right to emphasise the crucial importance of bringing down inflation; the current deep recession will achieve this. With continued high interest and sterling exchange rates we are going for overkill, with grave potential consequences for the economy of this country.

Where does this leave the pure monetary theory of inflation? Ultimately the rate of inflation will be governed by the quantity of money in circulation: but money has certain elastic properties. It has a habit, at least in the short run, of stretching into new forms of credit to meet new circumstances; this would be the case, for instance, where an increase in the cost of imports was associated with new forms of credit being provided by the exporting countries. What I am saying is that a policy of achieving world economic equilibrium through rigid world monetary policy based on fixed exchange rates, admirable though this may be in theory, is likely in practice to cause the type of political disruption that it is one of the quests of this book to avoid.

Nor is it reasonable to assert that the actions of governments in defense of the narrow interests they espouse will always have a wider or longer-term perverse effect. Those who would take away all power from politicians to influence the exchange rate argue, for instance, that governments, especially those of economically less successful nations, will engage in beggar-my-neighbor rounds of self-defeating devaluations of their currencies in order to protect their trade balances. I wonder.

Politicians on the whole have an aversion toward devaluation. It looks weak and like a sign of failure: and, of course, for a country heavily dependent on imports, for instance of raw materials, it can have perverse effects. In technical terms, if the price elasticity of demand for an imported commodity is low, a rise in its price to the importing country may actually increase the rate at which the latter has to pass its currency across the exchanges. What is more, subject to monetary policy, there may be an inflationary effect. In most cases there will be definite limits to the extent to which governments will wish to use devaluation as a protective device.

As for speculators, of course they will try to second-guess and to outsmart movements in exchange rates. They are most inclined to do so when currencies are artificially pegged to one another in a way that comes to be generally appreciated as unrealistic. This was, for instance, the situation in Europe in the early 1990s under the European Exchange Rate Mechanism, until the whole thing was blown apart in the early autumn of 1992.

A truly floating exchange rate system furthers the cause of free trade by providing a mechanism by which chronic trade and capital imbalances are brought back into equilibrium. True, it blurs relative efficiencies between different countries, but it also takes the fear out of trade.

The ideal world is where currencies gently float against one another, depending on marginal relative changes between the various economies. In such a world there are not many quick fortunes to be made by speculators, because the movements are too slow. Fig. 9, on page 75, shows that with respect to sterling, since leaving the Exchange Rate Mechanism the real world has not been too far off the ideal. In such a world the primary role of government will be to interfere as little as possible, in the knowledge (not possible in a fixed exchange rate system) that the trade markets will find their own equilibrium. What is required is that there should be no "pegs," no fixes between nations, no cartels, and above all no restrictive trade blocs leading to the artificial linking of currencies—not, that is, unless the links are the product of an amalgamation of several countries into one new nation-state; but that poses different issues.

The choice facing the West today is much the same as that which faced the Soviet bloc after World War II: between meeting head-on the challenge of world trade with the adjustments and the benefits that it will bring, or of attempting to shut out markets that are growing and where a dynamic new pace is being set for innovative production. The problem about the second approach is not simply that it won't hold: satellite technology alone will ensure that consumers will begin to demand those goods that the East is able to provide most cheaply. More fundamentally, it will guarantee the emergence of a fragmented world in which natural fears will be fanned and inflamed. A world divided into rigid trade blocs will be a deeply troubled and unstable place in which suspicion and ultimately envy will possibly erupt into a major war. I do not say that the converse will necessarily be true, that in a free trading world there will be an absence of all strife. Such a proposition would manifestly be absurd. But to trade is to become interdependent, and that is a good step in the direction of world stability. With nuclear weapons at two a penny, stability will be at a premium in the years ahead.

Fig. 10
AVERAGE MONTHLY EXCHANGE RATES

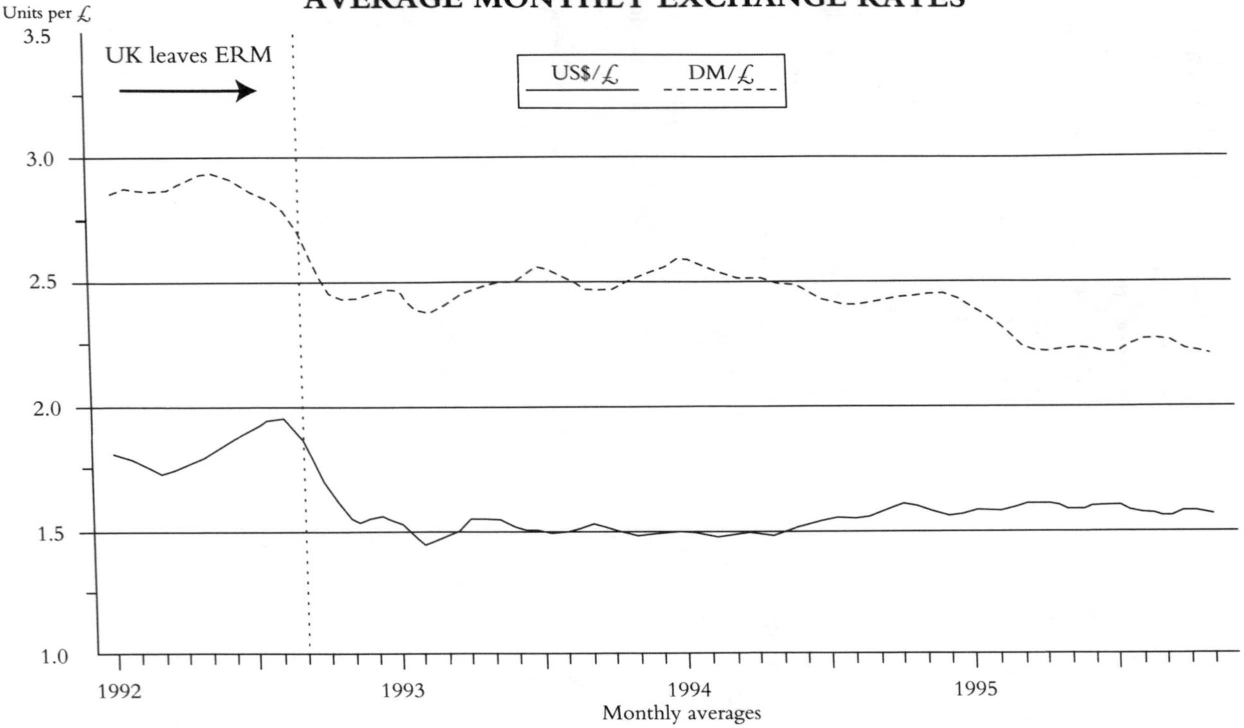

US$/£ ───── DM/£ ─ ─ ─ ─

UK leaves ERM

Units per £

3.5

3.0

2.5

2.0

1.5

1.0

1992   1993   1994   1995

Monthly averages

TRADE BLOCS TOWARD
FREE TRADE

Trade associations between Western countries make sense only in so far as they are stepping stones toward greater Western unity and total free trade. NAFTA and the South American trading arrangements can just about be defended as part of a process of pointing Trade Blocs toward free trade. The European Union, if it maintains its present course, cannot.

For all the reasons given in Chapter 4, Europe is heading toward becoming the most intensive, the most heavily protected, and the highest cost trade bloc ever and anywhere. If this comes about, it is likely that the Americas will feel bound to follow suit. The question, in the interest of preserving a freely trading and thus more prosperous and stable world, is whether there is anything that can be done to prevent this prospect for Europe from coming about. Is there a practical alternative to a protectionist centralist European superstate?

Since the summer of 1994, I have chaired an expanding group of European parliamentarians from twenty-four countries. Called the European Research Group, its members come from some thirty-five center-right parties. At the time of writing, we have met at Brasenose College, Oxford, the National Assembly in Paris, and the European Parliament building in Brussels.

Arising from these meetings, there has developed the concept of a Europe of "variable geometry." The term may seem rather formidable and off-putting; in essence its meaning is very simple: with the overriding objective of closer trade, and using the institutions and the legal framework of the European Union, the nations of Europe come together in a multiplicity of different arrangements that suit the varied needs of each country. The model is described in some detail in Appendix I, which reprints the text of the European Research Group's paper "A Europe of Nations," published in early 1995.

Member states pool policy-making powers only in those areas in which they see it as being in their interest to do so; for certain states this may involve border or environmental matters; others may wish to proceed with a common currency; others may come together on a single defense or foreign policy. Except on matters concerned with the development of free markets between European countries, it becomes a matter of choice for the individual nation as to how much sovereignty it surrenders to the common "pool." In mid-1995 the concept was formally put by the European Research Group to the Reflections Committee, which sits in Madrid and has been charged with the task of preparing an agenda for the Intergovernmental Conference beginning in 1996. The relevant section of the ERG paper read as follows:

A FLEXIBLE STRUCTURE

IV.   There must be a clearer definition of the division of powers between the Union and its Member States. The principle of subsidiarity is undermined by the difficulty of legal definition. The

Union should adopt as an alternative, to be enshrined in the Treaties, the principle that every Member State be allowed to administer for itself any policy which cannot be shown directly to affect the internal affairs of another Member State.

V. The Union need not apply its policies uniformly to every Member State. It is both undemocratic and impractical to force policy upon a nation against its wishes. The Union should apply to every Member State only those policies which by their nature require unanimous action, such as the maintenance of the Single Market.

VI. There should be no presumption that the powers of the Union will increase over time. On the contrary, powers should pass up and down from the Member States and the Union as necessary. The Union should be required constantly to prove that action at European level is needed in any area in which it acts; that is, that the policies of one Member State are directly affecting the domestic affairs of other Member States. The doctrine of the "occupied field" should be abandoned and the *acquis communautaire* made subject to continuous revision.

VII. In areas which do not require unanimous action, different groups of Member States should be able to come together under the aegis of the Union to collaborate on matters of common concern. Union structures should allow for flexible co-operation among different groups of countries. Any group of Member States wishing to pursue integration in an area which does not inherently require unanimous action should have recourse to the institutions, procedures and mechanisms of the Treaties. Member States choosing to retain national control of such policy areas would be unrepresented in the Union's institutions when those areas were under discussion.

A clear advantage of the "variable geometry" model in terms of the pursuit of free trade is that European countries would no longer be under an obligation to undermine their international trading positions by necessarily complying with the expensive social and bureaucratic costs imposed by membership of the European Union. Some member states might wish to maintain centrally imposed social conditions on their industries; others might not. Some might see advantages in linking their currencies to the Deutschmark; others might prefer to retain the freedom to manage their own exchange rates. It would be up to individual nations to choose on the basis of their perceptions of the true interests of their citizens.

Another trade benefit of greater choice and variety in the structure and workings of the European Union would be the removal of most of the barriers that currently exist to closer links between the EU and the former Soviet bloc countries. These are at present caused almost entirely by the European Union's insistence on an absolute compliance with a wide range of universally applicable conditions and rules.

The newly democratic countries of Eastern Europe will never be able to join the European Union in anything like its present form. Part of the problem is that membership of the European Union by the countries of Eastern and Central Europe would undermine the protectionist Common Agricultural Policy as presently constituted.

An even greater barrier is the plan for economic convergence and monetary union agreed at Maastricht. No one pretends that the Eastern and Central European countries will be able to meet Maastricht's economic criteria in the foreseeable future. Eastern Europe presents the EU with something of a dilemma. On the one hand the current policy of exclusion interspersed with grudging assistance cannot continue. It is untenable whether from an altruistic or a self-interested point of view, and makes likely a permanent division in Europe between a protectionist West and an unstable and resentful East. On the other hand, full membership of the Union for the Eastern countries is not a practical proposition under the current rules of the Union.

It is thus evident that new modes of association must be explored. There is certainly a strong mutual interest throughout Europe in adopting a common approach to such issues as border security, environmental protection, and, above all, defense. The former eastern bloc countries have made clear their urgent desire to be locked into some form of continental security system, and it is in the Community's clear interest to draw them into a democratic and peaceful European structure. The European Commission has shown some open-mindedness on the subject of variable integration. In 1991, Commissioner Frans Andriessen proposed a form of "affiliate membership," which "would provide membership rights and obligations in some areas while excluding others."

Eastward expansion will force the EU to acknowledge a truth it has so far avoided: that it is no longer realistic to demand a total acceptance of the *acquis communautaire* and the *finalité politique* from new members. Any kind of arrangement with Eastern Europe must be based on the principle that states are able to pool certain policies, even policy-making structures, in areas where they have a common interest, while retaining full sovereign control of others. Once established, this principle is likely to become the basis of a new European confederation. Both Eastern and Western European states should be able to select some fields of policy that they wish to administer within EU structures for mutual benefit, while retaining total control over others. This might involve sending ministers with full voting rights to some Council meetings while remaining outside others. Some states might choose to integrate their asylum policies, others their monetary policies or currencies, others their transport networks. Europe would, in effect, coalesce into a set of overlapping circles.

This new model is germane not only within an EU context but within a wider European framework. An unsettling development in recent years has been the EU's ambition to arrogate to itself the functions that lie within the domain of other organizations. There currently exists a clearly understood division of responsibilities in Europe: human rights abuses are the province of the Council of Europe; national minorities are dealt with by the Organization for Security and Cooperation in Europe (OSCE); defense is the business of NATO; and so on. There are both advantages and disadvantages in these arrangements. But the attempts by the Union to take over so many responsibilities have one particular drawback: they will make even more difficult the assimilation of non-EU countries into a European concert. In the Balkans and the Baltic states, in Central Europe and the CIS, countries with scant hope of admission to the Union set great store by their membership of the various pan-European bodies. If the functions of these bodies are agglomerated by the EU, this can only have the effect of accentuating the already dangerous divisions in Europe, widening the gap between EU member states and nonmembers.

The speedy integration of the nations of Eastern and Central Europe into a wide European confederation will be of great benefit to the states of Western Europe. It will draw them toward a looser and more sensible paradigm of European unity, a multifaceted Europe characterized by flexible and voluntary cooperation among groups of states within the constant nexus of a European free trade area.

There is already some precedent for the development of a consensual and many-tiered Europe. The Schengen Group, for example which allows for passport-free movement among some European countries, operates within EU structures without encompassing all member states; Greece never participated in the European Monetary System; above all, the Maastricht negotiations established the principle of integration without unanimity in the vital fields of social policy and monetary union. Already the more progressive elements in the Community have realized that it is both undemocratic and inefficient to force common policies on all member states, regardless of their popularity or practicability. The continuing political and geographical expansion of the Community will render unanimity quite untenable. It will simply not be possible to apply a Common Agricultural Policy to the north of Norway and to the citrus plantations of Cyprus; to offer common residence rights to Dutchmen and Turks; to impose common social costs on Danish and Slovak employers; to expect a common foreign and defense policy to embrace Switzerland and the United Kingdom. Insisting on unanimity can prevent the adoption of sensible pragmatic policies, dragging all states down to the lowest common denominator.

For this reason, there are signs that European commentators and politicians are beginning to raise their eyes from the model of European unity laid down forty years ago in circumstances very different from those of today. A new concept is beginning to emerge of a Europe of many circles, capable of integrating all the continent's nations and meeting the diverse wishes of their peoples. It is a vision of an expanded and powerful free trade zone, buttressed with close collaboration among its members in several areas; a many-layered Europe where groups of countries are able to come together to pursue common policies for mutual interest while retaining control over areas of solely domestic concern.

The 1996 Intergovernmental Conference will be an opportunity to restructure the Union so as to enable it to meet the challenge of establishing a multivariate Europe. In this context there are several aspects of the EU that would need to be reexamined, with a view to amending the treaties.

First, the balance of power among EU institutions would need to be re-formed to take account of legitimate aspirations for national democracy and the need for a more practical and decentralized decision-making process. The European Commission would lose its rights to initiate legislation. The number of commissioners would be reduced, as would their political status. Commission proceedings would be published and its members made accountable to national parliamentary committees. The Commission would, in short, be given a role more suitable to an unelected civil service. The European Court of Justice would be stripped of its growing legislative function, and would abandon the doctrine of direct applicability, which allows it to bypass national legal systems. Its members would be qualified judges who are confined to interpreting the specific legal disputes that arise from the treaties. The European Parliament would be given a clearly delineated function scrutinizing the Commission bureaucracy. The basic building block of democracy would be the national parliament, whose legitimacy as a lawmaking body is recognized by its electors. All this would leave the Council of Ministers as the chief instrument of European unity. It would absorb the executive and lawmaking powers of the other institutions and become the fulcrum of a flexible and intergovernmental paradigm of European cooperation.

Second, there would need to be a radical overhaul of the

Union's trade and agricultural policies. The Common Agricultural Policy is unsustainable in its present form. It places a heavy and unnecessary burden upon Europe's taxpayers and consumers. It is responsible for artificial hardship in the rural economies of Eastern and Central Europe, and is the direct cause of much terrible poverty in the Third World. It stands in the way of a properly liberal world trade regime and creates tensions among Europe's peoples. The principle of maintaining distorted food prices would need to be dropped, and the question of agricultural subsidies left to national governments. The EU might likewise move toward the abolition of the Common External Tariff and the adoption of a properly liberal approach to world trade, including the fields of agriculture, coal, steel, and textiles.

Third, the Union would need to extend the internal market so as to unlock Europe's economic potential. Free trade and competition ought to be extended as soon as possible to the fields of aviation, shipping, energy, and especially to insurance, banking, and investment services. The Commission's tacit policy of allowing protection to state-owned companies ought to be halted.

Fourth, European politicians must explore alternatives to economic and monetary union. The plan for economic convergence agreed to at Maastricht is being shown to be unworkable. It is not reasonable to expect the peoples of Europe's less wealthy areas to give up their natural advantages of low costs and competitive devaluation and become reliant instead on cohesion handouts from North European taxpayers; nor is it reasonable to expect these taxpayers to continue to underwrite an artificial convergence program. In a truly successful European economic area, a free exchange will ensure that the less developed regions are never allowed to fall too far behind: they will automatically price themselves back into the market.

Fifth, the European Union would need to work toward the immediate extension of elements of European integration to any state that wishes to participate in them. This would be far easier in a loose, consensual Europe. It is unrealistic to speak of a two-speed Europe. What is emerging is a multispeed Europe, with as many speeds as there are participating states. Indeed, even the notion of speed is a little misplaced, for it implies that the destination is fixed and only the rate of approach is variable. Would a country that participated in a common defense but retained its own currency be on a faster track than one that joined a single currency but remained outside a common security policy? It would be more accurate to talk, as did Strabo in antiquity, of a Europe of many shapes. Common policies in certain clearly delineated areas would be made available to all countries that shared a Western heritage. It should in time be possible to draw the United States, Canada, even Russia into a system of Western institutional cooperation based on such a European model.

Finally, there is the question of the location of power within the EU. I have suggested that every state would need to be allowed to administer for itself policies of solely domestic concern. These areas would be clearly defined and enshrined in a new treaty. Mechanisms would need to be put in place requiring the Community to prove that action at supranational level is necessary before it acts in any given area.

This is the model suggested by European history and culture. Western civilization is defined by plurality, democracy, diversity, entrepreneuralism, and individual liberty. These values should not be distorted in the name of European unity.

What practical hope is there of a model such as the one I have described being installed in Europe?

The 1996 Intergovernmental Conference of European Heads

of Government may come to be the last shoot-out between those forces that believe in a single federal United States of Europe and those who believe in a free association of sovereign nations. The combat will be more evenly matched than it has been in the recent past.

On the one hand, the federalists will be represented by some of the old-guard political leaders, such as Chancellor Kohl. Their position will be strengthened by the passionate support of officials, especially in the Commission, and by the momentum of the new law (based on three concepts: direct applicability; as-of-now effect, by which the judiciary acts as a nonelected legislature; and *acquis communautaire*, by which federalist laws are compounded). There is also the effect of the Treaty of Maastricht and, in particular, the process leading toward a single currency, which under Article 109j must be established by 1 January 1999.

Against these enormously powerful forces there are ranged one or two countervailing factors. The first of these is public opinion, which is increasingly anxious about an overrapid development toward a federal state. Second, a general reappraisal is being made of what had previously been thought "home truths": for instance, democracy is no longer seen to be enhanced by transferring powers from national parliaments to unelected centralized institutions; the merits of a large protected home market as against the freedom to trade worldwide has been questioned; the very basis of the formation of the Common Market—that the nation-state has been the cause of instability—is being reconsidered against the proposition that it was a pan-European fascist movement that was the true cause of World War II, the nation-state being the instrument for restoring stability and freedom; the single currency is increasingly being seen as unnecessary and as dangerous; in general, the idea that there is no alternative to a federal state of Europe is being deeply questioned. For instance, a MORI poll carried out in Britain between 17 and 21 November 1994 and a Finnid poll in Germany carried out between 31 October and 13 November 1944 showed 56 percent in Britain and 53 percent in Germany opposed to a single currency. By mid-1995 this figure had risen in Germany to an astonishing 70 percent.

Finally, there are the implications of the expansion of the European Union to include the former eastern bloc countries, whose membership will require a fundamental change to many of the arrangements of the European Union, in particular that of the Common Agricultural Policy.

The question is whether this changing public mood will be reflected in the political process in time to act as a brake on the current momentum toward a federal state.

In the 1950s, when the current attempt at European integration was launched, every mainstream democratic politician was in favor of the process. On the Continent, only Fascist and Communist political parties, for very different reasons, resisted European supranationalism. Britain, of course, was a slightly different case. Having come through the war with her institutions intact, she did not share in the widespread feeling that the old order had failed and must be replaced by a new supranational order. Where nationalism on the Continent had been tainted by Fascism and collaboration, British patriotism had been the focus of resistance against the Nazi threat. Linked by blood, trade, and culture to the New World, Britain was unwilling to join an exclusive and potentially introverted European bloc that was already displaying a tendency toward anti-Americanism. Nor could a country with Britain's commercial tradition easily reconcile itself to membership of a customs union with an external tariff wall designed to protect its least efficient producers.

Britain aside, the European political class wholeheartedly pursued the vision of a federal Europe. For the Socialists, Europe represented at a basic level the old aspiration of international solidarity. For the Socialists, also, a united Europe was an opportunity to apply common working conditions and social standards. Workers could be insulated from cheaper labor elsewhere in Europe as minimum common standards were extended. A German auto worker would not easily be undercut by a Spaniard if Spain had identical holidays, pension rights, working hours, and bargaining powers to his own. The ultimate aim was a common European minimum wage. This "social Europe" would, of course, still be uncompetitive in the wider world, but left-of-center parties believed that its size would allow it to cut itself off, to cocoon itself, as well as giving it a powerful voice in international trade negotiations.

The European design has always had the enthusiastic support of the political left. There are, of course, millions of ordinary left-wing voters who are deeply hostile to the unemployment caused by European monetary integration, concerned by the fraud and corruption of the European elites, and moved by the poverty that Europe's trade and agricultural policies cause in the Third World. But their views are not reflected by their political leaders. Social Democratic and Socialist parties have not only worked for closer integration at the national level but have attempted to align their own policies with each other, moving to create a pan-European Socialist party. The Socialist group in the European Parliament has been the focus of this process. Its symbol (a stubby-finger hand in Socialist-Realist style clutching a red rose) has *is* adopted by all its member parties, and its Europe likewise binding on its candidates in every men trade union movement in Europe has similarly b

tional. The European Trade Union Congress is increasingly in the business of proposing policy at European level, which the national trade union movements then support. There is a certain logic in all this. Europe appeals naturally to the left. The single greatest obstacle to meeting their social aspirations has been the threat of competition from less regulated and more efficient foreign labor, and the European process removes this obstacle by applying high social costs uniformly to Europe.

It is rather more difficult to explain the acquiescence of the right-of-center parties in the march to federalism. One might have thought that the main pillars of conservatism—patriotism, personal freedom, small government, allegiance to trusted and cherished institutions—would all be undermined by the growth of a bureaucratic superstate.

To understand the right's former enthusiasm for Europe, it is again necessary to recall the political situation at the end of World War II. In every Continental state, right-wing politics had to some degree become associated with Nazism and its puppet dictatorships. The two major groups perceived to have organized resistance against Hitler were the left and the churches. As postwar politics assumed their shape, it was the political wing of the churches, the Christian Democrats, which became the main anti-Socialist force.

Of course there were some exceptions. In Britain, which had emerged from the war undefeated, and in France, where de Gaulle's looming presence dominated politics, ordinary right-wing parties survived. Elsewhere, however, the Christian Democratic movement expanded to straddle the center and the right.

The Christian Democrats were the heirs of the confessional the later nineteenth century. In Italy and Germany, tree led back directly to the political movements that

TRADE BLOCS TOWARD
FREE TRADE

TRADE ASSOCIATIONS BETWEEN Western countries make sense only in so far as they are stepping stones toward greater Western unity and total free trade. NAFTA and the South American trading arrangements can just about be defended as part of a process of pointing Trade Blocs toward free trade. The European Union, if it maintains its present course, cannot.

For all the reasons given in Chapter 4, Europe is heading toward becoming the most intensive, the most heavily protected, and the highest cost trade bloc ever and anywhere. If this comes about, it is likely that the Americas will feel bound to follow suit. The question, in the interest of preserving a freely trading and thus more prosperous and stable world, is whether there is anything that can be done to prevent this prospect for Europe from coming about. Is there a practical alternative to a protectionist centralist European superstate?

Since the summer of 1994, I have chaired an expanding group of European parliamentarians from twenty-four countries. Called the European Research Group, its members come from some thirty-five center-right parties. At the time of writing, we have met at Brasenose College, Oxford, the National Assembly in Paris, and the European Parliament building in Brussels.

Arising from these meetings, there has developed the concept of a Europe of "variable geometry." The term may seem rather formidable and off-putting; in essence its meaning is very simple: with the overriding objective of closer trade, and using the institutions and the legal framework of the European Union, the nations of Europe come together in a multiplicity of different arrangements that suit the varied needs of each country. The model is described in some detail in Appendix I, which reprints the text of the European Research Group's paper "A Europe of Nations," published in early 1995.

Member states pool policy-making powers only in those areas in which they see it as being in their interest to do so; for certain states this may involve border or environmental matters; others may wish to proceed with a common currency; others may come together on a single defense or foreign policy. Except on matters concerned with the development of free markets between European countries, it becomes a matter of choice for the individual nation as to how much sovereignty it surrenders to the common "pool." In mid-1995 the concept was formally put by the European Research Group to the Reflections Committee, which sits in Madrid and has been charged with the task of preparing an agenda for the Intergovernmental Conference beginning in 1996. The relevant section of the ERG paper read as follows:

A FLEXIBLE STRUCTURE

IV.   There must be a clearer definition of the division of powers between the Union and its Member States. The principle of subsidiarity is undermined by the difficulty of legal definition. The

reflect their anxieties, they will turn to extremist fringe parties or lose faith altogether in the democratic process.

So, what are the portents for a fresh start being made at the Intergovernmental Conferences opening in 1996?

Without doubt, Germany and France in their different ways and from differing perspectives are each beginning to have second thoughts about the pace and direction of developments in the European Union. Germany is becoming increasingly anxious about the prospect of sacrificing her currency. France is less happy than she was about surrendering sovereignty over such matters as foreign policy, defense, and immigration policy; her new president, Jacques Chirac, is mindful of the fact that the Treaty of Maastricht was supported by only the narrowest of margins in the referendum of 1992.

Portrayed invariably as the odd man out, Britain may yet play a pivotal role in determining the future of Europe. As I argued in a submission made in early 1995 to the House of Lords on behalf of the European Research Group (Appendix II), Britain as a heavy net contributor to the EU budget (some 2 billion pounds a year) and as a large net purchaser of goods and services (some 10 billion pounds a year from other EU countries) has a strong negotiating position should she decide to use it.

Britain has an especially strong interest in ensuring that the EU does not drag her into a protectionist morass. Per head of population, Britain remains among the foremost trading nations of the world, far outranking Japan, for instance. Her high dependence on trade means that Britain cannot afford for long to be party to a process of creating a centralist, protectionist trade bloc. Unless a more flexible arrangement is found for the European Union, based on the principle of free trade and free association, it is hard to see how Britain could indefinitely remain a fully paid-up member of it. Britain's destiny is to trade with Europe, of course; but it is also, more urgently, to tighten her commercial links with the fast-growing countries of the Orient and with the large and familiar markets of the Americas.

Britain may act as a catalyst to the shaping of a newly outward-looking, free-trading Europe, or she may fail in this task. In the latter case, she would probably decide to plow her own way, as she has done so often and so successfully in the past on the high seas and in the open skies, unshackled by the weight of European bureaucracy and regulations. Her willingness to take this course may itself turn out to be the strongest card she has to play in determining the future shape of Europe.

The flashpoint for Britain will be the moment of decision—probably in 1998—about whether or not she should join the single currency. Her opt-out from this aspect of the Maastricht Treaty left the matter open. It is inconceivable that a British government of whatever political complexion would take the decision to join the single currency without reference to a referendum.

Britain's success or failure in helping to direct Europe onto the route of flexibility and free trade will depend in part on the intrinsic merits of her case. In order to judge these I need next to explore the global implications of what transpires in Europe. How important for the peace and stability of the world is it that Europe should be prevented from launching a chain reaction of protectionist trade blocs? To what extent does the peace of the world really depend on global free trade?

seek consensus with the left. The right in its purer forms of conservatism and classical liberalism stands for none of these things.

Conservatives oppose the aim of a federal Europe because of a belief in sovereignty, national identity, and the maintenance of familiar institutions. They are naturally suspicious of a project that is at once Utopian and Socialist in its conception. Liberals are against a federal Europe because they associate it with bureaucracy, regulation, uncompetitiveness, intrusiveness, and restrictions on personal freedom. They do not wish to see state control imposed from an even higher level, nor do they wish to be part of a protective customs union. Like conservatives, they have no stomach for compromise with an essentially left-wing organization.

As the right separates out into these two elemental forms, the peoples of Europe will at last be offered politicians who reflect their aspirations for the European Union. Outside the palaces and chancelleries of the Continent, Europe was for a long time a matter of no interest. Since the Maastricht debates of 1992, however, people have become increasingly aware of how European integration affects their lives. Whole groups of Europeans have seen their livelihoods threatened: Breton fishermen chafing under the Exchange Rate Mechanism (ERM), Portuguese port makers hampered by pettifogging regulations, British homeowners impoverished by the ERM, German taxpayers, unemployed Spaniards. The voters of Europe are turning against the federal process, in referendums, opinion polls, and elections, in a way that has shocked their political leaders.

In some countries, like Portugal, Spain, and Italy, there has been a change in the policy and composition of center-right parties; in others a wide and potentially dangerous rift has opened up between politicians and their constituents. The concern in this case must be that if people cannot find mainstream politicians to

Berlusconi swept to power on an unashamedly right-wing ticket. Some of the support for the Christian Democrats had shifted to the National Alliance led by Gianfranco Fini, whose origins went back to a party founded by supporters of Mussolini. The majority, however, switched to Mr. Berlusconi's *Forza Italia*, a populist movement offering Italy a strong cocktail of low taxes, open markets, decency, and patriotism. At the time of writing, the remnants of the Christian Democrats, now called the Italian Popular Party, command around 5 percent of popular support.

The shock waves from Italy have been felt by Christian Democrats around Europe. In Portugal, the CDS abandoned its long-standing constitutional commitment to be a party of the center and changed its name to Popular Party. At the same time, it too adopted an unequivocally right-wing manifesto, pledging itself to massive privatization and deregulation, the repeal of Maastricht and of the commitment to monetary union, and a new emphasis on Portugal's former colonies. The Spanish center-right has also shed its centrism and begun to advocate a program of radical market liberalism, national unity, trans-Atlantic ties, and opposition to a federal Europe. In Austria the Christian Democrats (called the Austrian Peoples Party) have been drubbed at the polls as their supporters begin to switch in large numbers to the right-wing Freedom Party. Even in the Low Countries support for Christian Democracy has waned, with the Dutch party suffering its worst defeat in living memory. Christian Democracy, once the dominant political force in Western Europe, now seems secure only in Germany.

The importance of this development in the context of this book cannot be overstated. Christian Democracy is a doctrine characterized above all by support for a regulated social market, by belief in a United States of Europe, and by a willingness to

Britain aside, the European political class wholeheartedly pursued the vision of a federal Europe. For the Socialists, Europe represented at a basic level the old aspiration of international solidarity. For the Socialists, also, a united Europe was an opportunity to apply common working conditions and social standards. Workers could be insulated from cheaper labor elsewhere in Europe as minimum common standards were extended. A German auto worker would not easily be undercut by a Spaniard if Spain had identical holidays, pension rights, working hours, and bargaining powers to his own. The ultimate aim was a common European minimum wage. This "social Europe" would, of course, still be uncompetitive in the wider world, but left-of-center parties believed that its size would allow it to cut itself off, to cocoon itself, as well as giving it a powerful voice in international trade negotiations.

The European design has always had the enthusiastic support of the political left. There are, of course, millions of ordinary left-wing voters who are deeply hostile to the unemployment caused by European monetary integration, concerned by the fraud and corruption of the European elites, and moved by the poverty that Europe's trade and agricultural policies cause in the Third World. But their views are not reflected by their political leaders. Social Democratic and Socialist parties have not only worked for closer integration at the national level but have attempted to align their own policies with each other, moving to create a pan-European Socialist party. The Socialist group in the European Parliament has been the focus of this process. Its symbol (a stubby-fingered hand in Socialist-Realist style clutching a red rose) has been adopted by all its member parties, and its European manifesto is likewise binding on its candidates in every member state. The trade union movement in Europe has similarly become supranational. The European Trade Union Congress is increasingly in the business of proposing policy at European level, which the national trade union movements then support. There is a certain logic in all this. Europe appeals naturally to the left. The single greatest obstacle to meeting their social aspirations has been the threat of competition from less regulated and more efficient foreign labor, and the European process removes this obstacle by applying high social costs uniformly to Europe.

It is rather more difficult to explain the acquiescence of the right-of-center parties in the march to federalism. One might have thought that the main pillars of conservatism—patriotism, personal freedom, small government, allegiance to trusted and cherished institutions—would all be undermined by the growth of a bureaucratic superstate.

To understand the right's former enthusiasm for Europe, it is again necessary to recall the political situation at the end of World War II. In every Continental state, right-wing politics had to some degree become associated with Nazism and its puppet dictatorships. The two major groups perceived to have organized resistance against Hitler were the left and the churches. As postwar politics assumed their shape, it was the political wing of the churches, the Christian Democrats, which became the main anti-Socialist force.

Of course there were some exceptions. In Britain, which had emerged from the war undefeated, and in France, where de Gaulle's looming presence dominated politics, ordinary right-wing parties survived. Elsewhere, however, the Christian Democratic movement expanded to straddle the center and the right.

The Christian Democrats were the heirs of the confessional parties of the later nineteenth century. In Italy and Germany, their pedigree led back directly to the political movements that the Roman Catholic Church had encouraged as an alternative to Socialism for the working classes. The hallmarks of Christian Democracy are consensus, solidarity, and moderation. Drawing support from both employers and trade unionists, the Christian Democrats encouraged dialogue and consensus in industrial relations,with workers' boards and committees. They were comfortable with the concept of a social market economy. Their approach to economic policy was derived ultimately from the papal encyclical *Rerum Novarum* of 1892, which laid down the rights and duties of workers and employers that were needed if harmonious relationships were to be assured. As the welfare state emerged from the ruins of World War II, Christian Democrats were able to reflect the prevailing zeitgeist by accepting and extending the machinery of state control and social intervention, machinery so central to the development of the EU.

Along with a distaste for the unfettered free market, Christian Democrats were suspicious of national sovereignty. Their movement was descended from political Catholicism, and they were accustomed to the idea of supreme authority above the nation-state. The appeal of a united European Christendom had a romantic appeal that harked back to the Middle Ages. Like the Socialists, European Christian Democrats not only worked to hasten the process of European unity but partly merged their parties at European level to hasten the process. The European Peoples Party is the pan-European organ of Christian Democracy, running candidates on a common manifesto and moving to become a truly transnational party.

The Christian Democrats owed their initial postwar predominance to being the only powerful and organized non-Socialist resistance to Nazism. They retained it by being seen as the best way to contain the Communist menace. When the Cold War was at its height, the European left was seen as a potential Soviet Trojan horse. Christian Democracy was a way of uniting all respectable non-Socialist sections of society around policies that would maintain spending on defense and support the NATO alliance. With its appeal to Christian values and its offer of strong rights for workers, Christian Democracy remained the most effective way to prevent the working classes from falling to the left.

The fall of the Berlin Wall robbed Christian Democrats of the anti-Communism that had been so central to their ideology. Fear of the red menace had been more important to them than they realized. There was now little appetite for a bland, even anemic, creed whose main attraction had been its ability to appeal to all non-Socialists. The price for this universality of appeal had been a certain lack of ideological consistency.

With the Communist menace gone, the European right began to dissolve into its two natural constituent forms, conservatism and classical liberalism. There was no need to appeal to the center anymore. More important, the assumptions that had underpinned the rise of the welfare state in the 1950s were being challenged. Privatization, deregulation, and small government were defining the new zeitgeist, and the function of the right was no longer seen as being to administer a social market in broad consensus with other parties. Since the mid-1980s, there has been increasing demand for a radical and principled alternative to Socialism.

The waning of Christian Democracy has affected almost every European country during the 1990s. The most extreme case is Italy. There, the Christian Democrats had been a part of every government since the late 1940s. The largest party at national and municipal level, and with representatives in every cabinet, they effectively ruled Italy for half a century. In 1994, they were extinguished as a political force. An alliance of parties under Silvio

CHAPTER EIGHT

WHAT HOPE FOR DEMOCRACY IN THE EAST?

WE HAVE REACHED the hub of the matter: is free trade of necessity the basis for world stability? In other words, are the benefits of free trade, crucially, political as well as economic?

At one level the answer is almost a truism. Trade means dialogue and—more important—interdependence. Arguing, as I have, that a mixture of capital and trade flows will be relatively balanced, under conditions of genuinely free trade, it is not unreasonable to suggest that the process will help rather than hinder the breaking down of barriers of mutual mistrust.

It goes further than that. Trade and war are on occasions direct alternatives to each other. If, for instance, China continues to have a growing problem with feeding her citizens, she will have the option to import food and the necessity to pay for this through exports; or she may develop expansionist claims over food-providing neighbors.

All this having been said, it would spoil the argument to be totally starry-eyed about the potential effects of trade on world peace and stability. The fact is that there is a great and growing political, cultural, and psychological divide between East and West. It exists irrespective of the level of trade between the two. Trade may act as a bridge, but it cannot on its own break down the barriers. For this to happen, certain other forces must come into play.

The first of these, and crucial, is for there to be a restoration in the West of a faith in the universal verity of its own principles, especially in those that relate to human rights. If the West lacks confidence in itself, it will be defensive and mistrustful of others. Conversely, faith in its own values will lead it to insist on certain minimum democratic standards and practices, the absence of which in major countries will lead to permanent instability in international relations.

Second, there will need to be acceptance by the West that the models of democracy arising in the East are likely to be very different from those of the West. Their emergence already in certain countries is a cause for optimism and an added reason for maintaining the pressure for basic human rights in the East.

In this context, there are several possible alternative approaches open to the West. The first is to persist with the view that Western culture, and the political and legal institutions that go with it, are part of the law of nature and of a common humanity. In this case the proper course of action will be to relax and to wait for the others to come round. Since at the end of the day we are all the same, the time will come of its own accord when all barriers will be broken down; we will then read one economic textbook and live under much the same parliamentary and legal system.

The problem with this strategy is that it flies in the face of the fact that differences between cultures are real, deep-rooted, and probably permanent. Even as the West reached the apex of its ascendancy, Islam was registering a new vibrancy, as were the teachings of Confucius.

Perhaps I might be permitted to indulge in one anecdote that certainly helped to fashion my interest in the differences between East and West. One warm spring evening in Nanjing I was sitting in almost total darkness in the backseat of a big black 1950s limousine. The curtains had been pulled tightly shut, presumably to ensure that the people outside might not glimpse the sight of a British politician in close conversation with the vice governor of the province of Jiangsu. The date was Wednesday 6 May 1987, and my companion was Mr. Chen Huanyou. It was a time, before the massacre at Tiananmen Square and immediately after the signing of the Sino-British treaty on Hong Kong, when relations between Britain and China were cordial, verging on warm.

My mission in China, as Britain's minister for aviation, was to secure Chinese compliance with an "open skies" policy for Hong Kong. The idea, simple and straightforward to me, was that by establishing the free flow of flights (subject only to genuine safety conditions) in and out of the colony, Hong Kong would become the aviation hub of the East. This would bring untold riches of trade and investment to the city and, through its gateway, to the whole country of China. British aviation interests would benefit through the significant position held in the market by British Airways and by Cathay Pacific.

When he had heard what I had to say, the man beside me sat in silence for a moment. I could not see his eyes because he wore dark glasses, despite the shaded windows. When he spoke, it was in slow but accurate English. He began by telling me something I already knew, that in addition to his overt official duties in and around Nanjing, he was a leading member of the recently established shadow government in Hong Kong. What he said, in effect, was that neither I nor the so-called sinologists at the Foreign and Commonwealth Office had the slightest clue as to the true nature of the Chinese mind. "Open skies" was for him not only an unattractive idea but, more significantly within the pattern of Chinese thought, a meaningless concept. In so far as he understood what it meant, it seemed to portend anarchy and confusion. At best it would give further prestige to Hong Kong, which was undesirable. When his government took over at the end of June 1997, Hong Kong would revert to its proper place as a small stone in the rich and vast mosaic of China, whose origins dated back mystically to the beginning of time and whose onward progress had no foreseeable end. Hong Kong would need to take its place humbly alongside Sanghaig, Quanzhou, Beijing, and even Nanjing. In the short to medium term, by which he seemed to mean at least the next fifty years, the pace of growth of Hong Kong would in all probability actually need to be slowed down.

At the time I put all this down to passing Communist rhetoric. I was wrong, of course; it went much deeper.

For much of human history, the Occident and the Orient have gone their separate ways, each leaving the other to its own devices. From time to time each has made a foray into the other's territory, from the adventures of Ghengis Khan to Western involvement in the Opium Wars. Despite the depth, the reality, and the power of the respective cultures, there has been little real competition between them—no lasting or overt threat that the one has posed to the other, either commercially, culturally, or ideologically. The Japanese have, of course, throughout the twentieth century made themselves felt in the West—and there are questions that will have to be asked about which side of the cultural divide Japan stands on. But what went on in China was as remote to the residents of

London as was the development of the American Constitution to the Manchurian warlords. Even the great wars of the twentieth century were, so far as the Chinese people were concerned, localized to quite distinct theaters within China.

Suddenly all this is changing. For the first time East and West may be heading on a definable collision course. Partly through newly emerging economic rivalries, partly through political differences, the cultural divide has become more sharply delineated. The threat is that this divergence translates itself into a more permanent form of hostility with very specific global implications.

It is as well to appreciate that the cultural differences between East and West are real and that they have specific implications for the way that each must react to the other. For Westerners to sit back and wait for the East to come their way may mean a long wait. It would be a response based on unreality, which is always a dangerous way forward in the conduct of human affairs.

The second possible response by the West to the "threat" of the East is for it to retreat behind protective walls. Much of this book has been devoted to making out the case against this approach. The very real danger is that this will indeed be the main thrust of the response by the West to the challenge from the East. Its effect economically will merely be to postpone the blast of competition when the barriers crumble and collapse from the pressure of consumer demand. Protectionism, as advocated by the founding fathers of the European Common Market, did not work against American competition any more than it would work against the East. The most vociferous champions of protectionism in Europe have in mind above all to save the high-technology industries, and it is precisely these, after many years of cosseting, that are currently in Europe lagging almost out of sight behind those of the Americans and the Japanese.

An even more profound and serious effect of protectionism will be to remove the political benefits of interdependence. If there are rivalries and mutual distrust, what better way to mollify them than by trading, and what could be more foolish than to sever commercial relations? A better way has to be found by the West of relating to the East than that of cutting itself off from it.

The answer to a competitive challenge is neither to pretend it does not exist nor to try to build temporary walls against it. The answer is to meet it head-on, to recognize the challenge for what it is, to rekindle a confidence in one's own values, to muster all available instruments, and to engage.

To accept that there are real and permanent differences between East and West is not to concede that the cultural values of the East are in any sense "better." On the contrary, it is nothing to be ashamed of to believe with passion that man was made for his own self-fulfillment and that through his personal achievements he may assist in the process of fulfilling the lives of those around him. Far from being a cause of self-doubt, it is a matter of pride to believe that man is in a state of grace when he is free. Far from bowing to them, we should challenge at every turn cultures that lead to the suppression of human individuality. To accept that there are competing cultures is not to accept that the other is right. Recent British policy in Hong Kong has been absolutely correct to uphold Western democratic virtues and to do her best up to the point of departure to ensure that they are applied.

The essential question is whether this competition between very different cultures can be conducted in peace into the next century. This will depend on whether there is the necessary modicum of compatibility between the belief systems. Is it possible to define a mutually acceptable meeting point, a bottom line that equates with both Western and Eastern cultures?

Can, in other words, the Confucian, Muslim, and Judeo-Christian traditions live together? The compatibility of human rights and the "Eastern way" has long been under question and with some reason. Few Eastern countries have, until recently, paid much attention to the needs of democracy, despite the fact that the 1948 United Nations Universal Declaration of Human Rights was devised by a committee of eight, which included a Chinese.

This has led some observers in the West to conclude that any insistence on a modicum of democracy is to push arrogantly at impregnable cultural barriers. They have gone on to argue that since Western definitions of democracy and human rights are too narrow, they need to be reshaped to suit the demands of Eastern culture. "Reshape" has become a euphemism for "abandon."

From the point of view of world stability, this line of thought poses grave problems. If the East is permitted to abandon all democratic standards, it is impossible to see how there can be any meeting point between the cultures. If the East poses an absolute threat to all human liberties, there can be no real peace with the West.

It is therefore necessary to be very clear about the minimal level of democracy that is acceptable to both East and West. The classical Western definition of democracy is that of S. M. Lipset. In *Political Man* (1960) he wrote: "Democracy in a complex society may be defined as a political system which supplies regular constitutional opportunities for changing the governing officials, and a social mechanism which permits the largest possible part of the population to influence major decisions by choosing among contenders for office."

It is this definition of democracy that requires some form of regular elections from a choice of contestants for office which many argue is too tough for the Eastern way. They suggest, for instance, that it should be watered down to ensure merely that the regime is "acceptable" to those under its rule. The problem is that without "constitutional opportunities for changing the governing officials," there is no obvious way of putting the "acceptability" of the government to the test. Referendums and polls may have their place in certain circumstances but they are of limited value as part of a permanent system of accountability.

The significance of ensuring genuinely proven acceptability is that only when the system of government is acceptable—including the means by which power is transferred—will its stability be perceived by other countries; and it is only when it is thought to be stable will there be confidence that its conduct of foreign policy will be rational. In other words, the level of democracy determines the confidence with which other governments can do business with it. More than this, mutual acceptance of each other's regimes means that everyone is to a greater extent on the same side; there is no fear on the part of one nation of being attacked by another with totally different ideas on basic democratic rights. What is more, history suggests that a stable regime, one that enjoys popular support, is less likely to be militarily aggressive than an unpopular dictatorship flying under whatever ideological or cultural banner.

We are therefore, I believe, stuck, even at a minimalist level, with Lipset's definition of democracy; anything much less will not do. Nor is it necessary that it should. Dr. Nihal Jayawickrama of Hong Kong University's Law Department has put the matter like this: "The problem [with Asian countries] is that their systems of government are not compatible with their constitutions, not that their cultures are incompatible. The basic premise of government must be that it is based on the will of the people" (*London Sunday Telegraph*, 6 March 1994).

The question arises as to what should be the position of Western countries when they are faced, as they are with present-day China, with a country that wants to do business with them but that manifestly does not comply with the minimum standards of democracy and human rights.

In these circumstances, considerations of free trade should prevail; but they should do so in a manner by which the West does not falter in its confidence in the values associated with democracy. Nor should the West refrain from a tireless and proactive effort to proselytize these values from a position of economic, political, and military strength.

The reasoning behind this is as follows: More trade provedly means greater all-around wealth, which itself generates the purchasing power for yet more trade. Where there is an imbalance of trade, the benefits, as a matter of generality, will accrue to the exporting organizations of the country in surplus and to the consumers of the country in deficit. Even in this crude case, there will be an increase in wealth on each side.

Recent detailed empirical studies in 125 countries have shown that democracy is positively correlated with per capita income levels.★ The richer a country is the more likely it is to register democratic tendencies.

What this means is that there is a benign circle linking free trade with democracy leading through the breaking down of mistrust between nations and cultures to a more harmonious and prosperous world.

The problem for the West is that there remains a gap—a wide

★John F. Helliwell of Harvard University used Gastil's and Bollen's *Indices of Political Freedom* to show "that there are no positive effects of democracy on economic growth" but that there was a strong positive causal effect of income on democracy. *Empirical Linkages between Democracy and Economic Growth* (Cambridge University Press, 1993).

one—between the political aspirations for free trade and their application in practice.

The fact is that in most of the world, certainly outside the Americas, Europe, and Japan, any movement toward democracy remains very faint indeed. The relationship between economic progress and political liberalism, however tenuous in some countries, does nevertheless just about hold as a general truth.

Of the world's thirty-nine Islamic states, only Turkey boasts a properly liberal democratic polity, with Malaysia, Pakistan, and Bangladesh qualifying if the criteria are not applied too harshly. Among the two dozen Confucian-type states of East Asia, Western-type political systems are confined to Japan, South Korea, to a lesser extent Taiwan, and, perhaps a little incongruously, Mongolia. The situation in sub-Saharan Africa is truly dire. Of the forty-one non-Muslim states in that continent, only Benin, Botswana, Cape Verde, and Mauritius have anything approaching a free and democratic system of government, with South Africa and Namibia as recent and welcome additions to their ranks. Among the other African states, political suppression, corruption, and a total disregard for human rights are common.

The fall of Communism has not been like the breaking of some great dam, allowing a flood of Western liberal capitalism to fertilize the parched fields of Africa and Asia. It was always unrealistic to assume that other models of government, some resting on ancient civilizations, would simply be washed away before a political system that has never truly existed outside the West. Nor is the reluctance to adopt a Western-liberal model wholly attributable to the inertia of current regimes. On the contrary, exponents of more authoritarian styles of government justify themselves by drawing on a cohesive anti-Western philosophy.

In the Confucian states, we are told that there is a special "Asian

Way," which eschews Western notions of human rights and free opposition as threats to social cohesion and economic growth. When Confucius was asked about the art of government, he replied simply: "sufficient food, sufficient weapons and the confidence of the people."

In Islamic nations, too, there are those who are quick to explain the lack of democracy by pointing to special cultural circumstances. Islam has its own mechanism, they claim, in the *shura*, which urges those in power to consult their people before deciding how to act. Islam, which means "surrender," has never placed a strong emphasis on individual responsibility (as the Judeo-Christian tradition does), stressing instead the supreme importance of following God's rules as closely as possible. To leaders like Mahathir bin Mohamad of Malaysia, authoritarian government is not just a necessary condition for prosperity but a desirable end in itself.

In black Africa, defenders of the one-party system claim that it closely reflects precolonial tribal ways. Many of their arguments are no more than the sophistry of authoritarian rulers seeking a system of thought to justify their tyranny.

The plain fact is that the full panoply of a free society—the rule of law, private property, freedom of speech, an independent judiciary—has never properly existed in the greater parts of Asia and Africa. Elements of liberalism were introduced by the European colonial administrations, but very rarely did they outlast the departing regimes. The notion that countries outside the Western tradition must in time come to evolve into liberal polities has yet to be proved.

Given the force of Eastern, especially Confucian, philosophy, it is probable that Western models of democracy will never be transferable to the East. The question is whether it is possible to envisage a common denominator by which the Eastern and Western traditions can be brought, if not into harmony, at least into a stable relationship with each other. For the West, the bottom line must involve pluralism and choice in the transfer of power. Anything less is dictatorship, which down the ages has meant internal instability with the prospect of external aggression.

The question is, how realistic is such a position, particularly with respect to the countries of the Orient?

On the surface, the omens are not good. And yet a closer look at what is happening in the economically more mature countries like South Korea, Taiwan, and, of course, Japan may throw a different light on the matter.

The "Asian Way" to which many Oriental leaders subscribe found formal expression in the Bangkok Declaration on Human Rights of April 1993. In essence, the Bangkok Declaration challenged the West's assumption that its own notion of human rights was universal. It spoke of the need to "avoid the application of double standards" and called for human rights to be "encouraged by cooperation and consensus, and not through confrontation and the imposition of incompatible values." The tone of the document betrayed annoyance at the way in which the West judged other countries by its own mores and sought to bully them into accepting alien Western notions of human rights. Its signatories wanted to

discourage any attempt to use human rights as a conditionality for extending development assistance; emphasise the principles of respect for national sovereignty and territorial integrity as well as non-interference in the internal affairs of States, and the non-use of human rights as an instrument of political pressure; [and] reiterate that all countries, large and small have the right to determine their political systems, control and freely utilise their own resources and freely pursue their economic, social and cultural development.

The claim is that there is a valid alternative to multiparty pluralism and an obsession with the rights of the individual. A benevolent capitalist authoritarianism that stresses order, cohesion, and obligation is more in keeping with the heritage of the Confucian states. Filial duty, tolerance, hierarchy: these are values to elevate, even at the expense of personal freedom and privacy. In the pure Confucian tradition, the ruler is a link between the gods and the people. The legal code and the machinery of government exist not to safeguard individual rights but as a means for a benign government to control its potentially disorderly subjects.

Capitalism alone has so far proved unable to loosen the grip of the Eastern despotisms as it did that of the authoritarian governments of Europe and the Americas. Drawing on a tradition of obedience two and a half thousand years old, the Oriental regimes have so far succeeded in absorbing a transfusion of Western capitalism without diluting their authoritarian culture. We are witnessing the rise of states that are economically powerful without being politically free. The question is whether they will always remain in this position.

GIANT CHINA HAS been moving toward a capitalist economy since 1978 with no commensurate political reform. Much the same can be said of several of its economically more "advanced" neighbors.

Lee Kuan Yew, who has taken to defending China's human rights record against "arrogant" attacks from the United States, was the effective founder of the state of Singapore, arguably the most Westernized and capitalist country in Southeast Asia. Yet Singaporean society, to Western eyes, is stiflingly oppressive. While elections of a sort are held, dissent is officially and unofficially discouraged, and the ruling People's Action Party holds seventy-seven of the island's eighty-one seats. Lee, who recently relinquished the premiership to become a roving elder statesman across East Asia, has become a stern critic of Western society, which he sees as plagued by crime and social breakdown.

Lee Kuan Yew and his allies in the ASEAN states were the first to seek to reintegrate China into world affairs after the terrible massacre in Tiananmen Square on 4 June 1989. Diplomatic ties were resumed in 1990 and ministerial visits exchanged. Before long, Lee was castigating the West for its haughtiness toward China when its own house was in such disorder. China, like Singapore, might offend Western liberal sensibilities by its harsh authoritarianism; but it was at least an ordered, decent society without drugs, pornography, or vandalism, where people walked the streets without fear and respected their elders.

In November 1990, Lee delighted the Beijing administration by telling the people of Hong Kong to grow up and forget the nonsense of direct elections. If they were to survive beyond 1997, he told them, they must strengthen their economic usefulness to China, not make themselves a nuisance by demanding representative government.

The Chinese government was naturally determined to make the most of Lee's support. In the aftermath of the Tiananmen murders, it had launched the slogan "Stability must prevail over everything." Now here was the leader of one of the wealthiest capitalist states in the region apparently agreeing. The *People's Daily* quoted Lee as pronouncing that political openness should not become the precondition for economic reform. The true prerequisite for economic growth, he argued, was order. Economic reform could not take place in the absence of social and political stability. The Chinese government immediately began to talk of a "Singaporean model" as a possible route to capitalism. It made much of the fact that Singapore's ethnically Chinese population had understood that growth could not exist without a strong government. Lee himself was quoted as saying that Chinese culture was a strong factor in his island's economic success. This accorded very conveniently with Beijing's campaign to promote Chinese values and traditions as an antidote to the Western "spiritual pollution" that was held responsible for the Tiananmen riots.

Lee Kuan Yew has been perhaps the most vocal critic of Western human rights in the region, but his sentiments were echoed in the aftermath of the 1989 massacre by the other ASEAN leaders. The Thai and Philippine governments began to mutter about Western arrogance, while Malaysia and Indonesia launched angry verbal crusades against the new moral imperialism. All ASEAN countries protested in strong language that the West should not use its economic strength to "blackmail" other countries into accepting its own values—that it should, in other words, continue to give economic aid to Asian countries regardless of their human rights abuses. Mahathir bin Mohamad of Malaysia reminded the West that precepts of human rights varied from country to country, and that in the developing world especially, individual rights should be balanced against economic growth and social cohesion. None of the ASEAN countries was itself above the violation of even the most basic human rights. The Tiananmen killings found their echo in the Indonesian government's massacre at Dili in November 1991 and in Thailand's brutal suppression of student protesters in May 1992.

The ASEAN states have done more than any other international association to work with China. China, for the most part, has responded with enthusiasm, wholeheartedly entering into the anti-Western rhetoric of the "Asian Way" and toying with elements of the ASEAN model as ideas for its own economic development.

The problem is to decide where all this will lead in the future. Are the current facts of suppression and the rhetoric that justifies it indications of endemic political systems that necessarily lie in conflict with the West? Or are there signs in the economically more advanced Asian countries that there may be room for compromise?

THE REPUBLIC OF China (Taiwan) has been the foremost enemy of the Chinese tyranny for half a century. Ever since its defeat and flight from the mainland, the Kuomintang has governed Taiwan in accordance with the teachings of Confucius and the Three Principles of Sun Yat-sen: nationalism, democracy, and well-being. While the regime has presided over astonishing economic growth, it remained totalitarian for many years. After the death of Chiang Kai-shek, who had led the Nationalist forces during the Chinese civil war, power passed to his son. The legislature (Yuan) was composed of aging Kuomintang MPs who had not seen their nominal mainland constituencies since the late 1940s. The native Taiwanese, who made up 85 percent of the population, were without representation. The Kuomintang itself was modeled on the Communist Party of the Soviet Union, with power concentrated in a Central Executive Committee (the equivalent of a Politburo). Taiwan flirted seriously with the USSR between 1946 and 1952, signing a friendship treaty. Nor did capitalism in Taiwan ever entirely follow the Western model; the state had a leading role in formulating economic strategy, and a form of technical nationalism was practiced. True to the Confucian tradition, capitalism was seen not as a way for the individual to reach his potential or as the logical consequence of property rights but rather as a means of enriching the state. Certainly it showed no signs in the early days of leading to political freedoms.

Then, in 1987, reforms began. Martial law was lifted, leading to the unbanning of strikes, demonstrations, and opposition newspapers. The Democratic Progressive Party was legalized, and allowed to contest elections. On 6 January 1993, in an event pregnant with symbolism, Kung Teh-cheng, the seventy-seventh direct lineal descendant of Confucius, stood down from his post in government. Reforms continued throughout the year. Lien Chan became the first native Taiwanese to become prime minister, while a reformist faction threatened to split the Kuomintang. Yet, at the elections which followed, the Kuomintang retained its overwhelming position. The blur between party and state had affected public attitudes in Taiwan as it had not in the once Communist states of Europe. The tradition of hierarchy in the East runs deep. The Kuomintang retained 102 parliamentary seats to the opposition's 52, and held on to its dominance of local government. Nevertheless, in Taiwan there may be emerging an "Asian Way" toward democracy.

LIKE TAIWAN, SOUTH Korea is another textbook example of capitalism and prosperity existing for decades without commensurate political reform. Like Taiwan, South Korea has only just moved to adopt a more democratic political system. In 1987, the Constitution of the Sixth Republic allowed more press freedom, guaranteed habeas corpus, and ensured the political neutrality of the army. Free elections were held the following year, and the ruling Democratic Justice Party was eventually defeated by the newly formed Democratic Liberal Party under the present president, Kim Young Sam. It would be quite wrong, however, to see elections in themselves as heralding the Westernization of South Korea. Administrative practices in Korea are often very arbitrary and personalistic. Accountability is, in many quarters, a novel and alien proposition. Such notions as impartial authority, equality before the law, respect for private property and the integrity of the person, rights of the minority, and due process have yet to make their way into the everyday routine of Korean life.

In the political sphere, the government continues to recoil from allowing the institutions of a truly pluralist society to develop. There has been little progress toward relinquishing the state's control of television, for example, or creating a truly independent judiciary.

The authoritarian governments of the 1960s and 1970s saw the key to economic growth as being the development of large conglomerates called *chaebol*, whose size allowed them to make colossal investments in plant and research and to set prices in collaboration with the government. Recently, small and medium companies have come to account for a large part of the South Korean economy, but these companies adopt a similarly acquiescent posture toward the government's guidance.

The symbiotic relationship between government and business has grown even closer in the last few years. Industrial strategy rests in the hands of the Ministry of Science and Technology and the Ministry for Industry, Trade and Energy—which between them have a function similar to that of Japan's Ministry for International Trade and Industry. One of the government's priorities is to discourage foreign imports and to subsidize exports. Another is to increase investment in research and development. This it does by a variety of means, including accelerated depreciation allowances, investment tax credits, deferral of income tax payments, and duty-free import of selected capital goods. There has been a particular emphasis on developing an ultrahigh technology capacity for Korea and on reversing the brain drain of scientists to Western laboratories. The ultimate aim is to reduce South Korea's dependency on foreign suppliers for technology. Thus, firms are being made increasingly self-reliant in areas such as microelectronics.

This kind of economic nationalism relies to a large degree on the Confucian obedience of the people, on their willingness to sacrifice personal economic gain in return for the perceived benefits of being part of a successful society. But it is also linked to a more direct kind of political nationalism. South Korea has recently made unprecedentedly strong demands for reunification with the North, even at the expense of links with the United States, its supposed ideological partner. There has even begun a rehabilitation of the late Kim Kung, the xenophobic postwar minister for Internal Security, who preached the doctrine of Korea's racial destiny and ridiculed the notion of limited government. This renewed interest in Korean unity reflects an increasing concentration on South Korea's ethnic identity (which links it with the North) over its political identity (which links it to the rest of the capitalist world).

In neither Taiwan nor South Korea has a free economy created a Westernized society; it is equally clear that democracy of a kind is now practiced in both countries; that is to say, systems are being established to provide for an element of choice of government and to legitimize the transfer of power; but free elections in themselves have not eroded the hierarchical and authoritarian traditions of ancient Confucian society. While it is too early to reach a judgment on the prospects for full pluralism in the Taiwanese and Korean Republics, it is possible to discuss in both countries the emergence of the basis for stable government with which the West can live at peace.

THE RELATIONSHIP THAT exists between the West and Japan provides the clearest model for the future. Japan, let there be no doubt, is an Eastern power. Hierarchical Confucian values permeate every sphere of Japanese life. In politics, every Member of Parliament is sponsored by interest groups, which he is expected to serve on a full-time basis throughout his career. A large percentage of Liberal Democratic constituencies have become effectively hereditary. The legal system appears to be heavily influenced by the Tokugawa era motto: "Let the people know nothing, but make them obey." The treatment of prisoners on remand is by Western standards outrageously oppressive and biased in favor of the presumption of guilt. The kind of debates advanced by Bentham or Rousseau about the nature of law and the state would be unintelligible to a Japanese Confucian legal philosopher. The notion of the law as a system open to the individual seeking redress rather than as a means for the state to ensure order is wholly alien to the Chinese Imperial Code and the Japanese system, which derives from it. Lawyers are very few in Japan and court cases rare. Court trials are seen as a loss of face for all concerned, and both parties will go out of their way to avoid them. On the rare occasions when a case does go to court, everything is done to avoid a clear-cut judgment giving victory to one side.

Oriental values pervade the functioning of Japan's capitalist economy. In the spirit of Confucian obedience, no company will challenge the Ministry for International Trade and Industry's (MITI's) official guidance. Indeed, the very rare occasions when a Japanese company has chosen to ignore government advice illustrate the astonishing powers of the state. One example will serve. In 1984, Taiji Sato, owner of a small Tokyo petrol retailer, attempted (perfectly legally) to import cheap refined oil from Singapore. MITI saw that this would undermine the carefully engineered cartel it had nurtured with the aim of preserving a Japanese refining capacity. With the backing—understandably—of the other petrol retailers, MITI bureaucrats prevented Sato from landing his petrol. Not content with this, they employed their contacts in the police and the foreign ministry to identify the financial institutions funding the company in Singapore and had their credit cut off to stop suppliers' selling the company the refined product. A court case would have been useless since the courts invariably align themselves with bureaucratic desires—even when MITI guidance appears to compel a company to break the law.

Where Western business is competitive, aggressive, Darwinian, Japanese business is cohesive, harmonious, prepared to sacrifice a short-term profit in order to build a long-term relationship with a grateful client. No Japanese firm will willingly sack an employee, whatever its economic prospects. Only during the last recession were a significant number of companies forced to lay off staff, and even then many preferred to offer them full wages and pension rights simply for not showing up for work. These arrangements struck Western observers as curious: employees were forbidden to work for a competitor, but could otherwise do whatever they wanted on full wages, including finding another job. Even stranger to Western eyes was the reaction of those offered this wonderful package: the vast majority turned it down, being unwilling to lose face by accepting redundancy. The fact is that Western economic principles do not apply very readily in Japan.

The real lesson to be learned from the Japanese experience is

that while Western models of democracy will in all probability
never be replicated in the East, a Confucian variant of a pluralistic
system of government is a perfectly practical proposition. It is
possible for Asian states to develop polities that are at once democratic and Confucian.

What is more questionable is whether political freedoms will
develop in the East without encouragement from the West. (Japan
had its form of government imposed on it in 1945.) The first
step must be for the West to reaffirm its belief in its own values.
On the back of renewed self-confidence, the West will need to
be firm without being simplistic in its relations with the East. The
British have been right, for instance, to state their determination to
leave behind a form of genuine democracy when they depart
Hong Kong in 1997—even though to have done so has been
apparently to irritate the Chinese and even more so the "old China
hands" in the Foreign and Commonwealth Office in London. To
have done otherwise would have been to have conceded that
democratic principles were negotiable. The governor of Hong
Kong, Christopher Patten, deserves great credit for his stance on
this matter. He has had to fight off powerful vested interests,
inside and outside Hong Kong, whose wish it has been to give
way to all Chinese demands. The policy of not doing so is right,
even if after 1997 China abandons much of what has been established. In the interests of world stability the West abandons the
principle of democracy at its peril. This is true even if in many
instances democracy remains an objective rather than the reality,
and even if on matters essentially of trade, the West must deal
with the reality. It is the central proposition of this book that
wherever there exists the option to maintain and to develop trade
it should be exercised. Where there is trade there is cause for

hope and belief that tyrannical regimes will be constrained, if not brought down.

The question of whether there exists the basis for a stable relationship between East and West pivots crucially on China. The unavoidable handicap in this relationship is that for the past four thousand years China has known only authoritarian government. Apologists for the present Chinese regime point out that China's *guoquing* ("national conditions") render it wholly unsuited to Western notions of democracy. It is true that in a country with well over a billion inhabitants, the distinction between dissent and anarchy is likely to be blurred. It is also incontrovertible that, as in the rest of Confucian Asia, the idea of a loyal opposition is regarded as a contradiction in terms.

It is equally clear that China is fast becoming a massive capitalist power. Her savings rates at 40% of GDP, twice the OECD average, her ability to channel these savings into productive investment and her low rates of taxation are understandably becoming the envy of much of the rest of the world. In Guangdong, economic reforms have led to the creation of a propertied middle class. In one village, Daquizhuang (near Tianjin), all households receive satellite television and most own at least one Mercedes. It is clear also that there exists in Chinese governing circles a greater concern than in Maoist times with moral questions associated with the right to rule. The resurrection of the teachings of Confucius—instanced in October 1994 at an international conference in Beijing to mark the sage's 2,545th birthday, an event that would have been unimaginable a few years earlier, is some evidence of a new sense in China of the *obligations* running in conjunction with the *rights* of government.

The world nevertheless holds its breath to find out whether a capitalist China will ultimately be a democratic China. The possibility that China might reach its full economic potential while retaining its totalitarian regime casts a dark shadow over world stability. Almost every one of China's contiguous states has felt the effects of its expansionist appetite: Korea, Mongolia, Tibet, Vietnam, Hong Kong, and above all Taiwan. China continues to nurse territorial claims upon a vast area of Siberia around Lake Baikal. She maintains that much of the South China Sea is her territory, causing anxiety in the Philippines; some Chinese scholars argue that a million square miles of Russian territory north of Mongolia are rightfully theirs. The Siberian land claimed is rich in natural resources and very sparsely populated. The contrast between the concentrated population of the Chinese North East and the almost empty stretches of Kamschatka across the border could not be more pronounced. A Chinese call for lebensraum lurks constantly beneath the surface.

China has come close to the limits of her cultivable land. Some 50 percent of the land bounded by the Tropic of Cancer and the South China Sea is in a degraded condition due to soil erosion and loss of vegetative cover. Dr. Lester Brown of the Washington-based Worldwatch Institute has argued that because her demand for food is outstripping her capacity to supply, China is suddenly losing the ability to feed herself. She has certainly become a net importer of raw materials. The facility with which she is able to trade will clearly become a heavy factor in determining the extent of her pretensions to expand her borders. Trade and war may in other words be very real alternatives for China. What is more, her trade patterns may either be open and spread freely across the world or they may be secretive and based on bilateral bartering with countries such as Iran and Iraq. In this case, the exchange is likely to take the form of oil for the supply by China of increasingly sophisticated, nuclear weaponry.

From the experience of the countries in East Asia one can, I think, draw these conclusions with respect to the future political regime of China: First, in East Asia, as in the Islamic world and in Africa, there are powerful cultural obstacles to the adoption of Westminster-style individualist democracy. Nor will Western values simply soak by themselves into these ancient civilizations.

Second, the grip on power of the illiberal governments in countries of Asia is not entirely secure. The West may have been less than successful in impressing the virtues of liberalism on the leaders of Asia and Africa, but the same is not necessarily true with respect to the peoples they rule. A boy growing up surrounded by American satellite television in Guangdong is perhaps less likely than his grandfather to accept meekly the authority of a repressive or unelected government. There is even talk of "de-Confucianization" as parents and teachers no longer enjoy quite the same reverential respect as they did for instance in Korea and Japan.

Third, the more confident the West is as to the links between free trade and democracy, and the more political stability is associated with economic progress, the more persuasive it is likely to be. Throughout history, nations have advanced by copying the most successful features of their neighbors. If the West demonstrates once more that its political and economic ideology brings tangible benefits, it may hope to convert others by its example.

As the world becomes richer and more interdependent through free trade, so there is a growing chance that political regimes will become more self-assured in terms of their domestic and international acceptability; there will be a tendency toward greater stability and lower tension, and a greater chance of ensuring world peace. If all this sounds a little starry-eyed, the converse is perhaps more plausible. As tension grows through a combination of poverty induced by trade restrictions, and as governments retain the capacity to build up their arms irrespective of their national wealth, so the likelihood of war grows.

General acceptance of a common denominator of external freedom (trade) and internal freedom (democracy) is the only basis for world equilibrium. These alone provide the necessary interdependence and mutual trust between states. One day a world body may provide the catalyst. That day is far off. In the meantime, only the West has the economic power and the experience to edge the world toward a stable state. If the West lacks the leadership and the sense of purpose to do it, there is no one else on the horizon who will.

What is required is a renaissance of Western self-confidence, which will be much more likely if there is a linking of arms across the Atlantic. The nations of Europe and of North America are at their best when they work in unison with the other. Rather than sniping at each other, let alone forming trade blocs against each other, they must join forces in the search, not for a new world order—that will continue to be a utopian dream—but for a mechanism for continually reducing tension. The West must throw away its self-doubt and vigorously promote an interrelationship between nation-states based on democracy and trade. It is the only way to accommodate the real and increasing rivalry that exists between the world's differing cultural systems.

The necessary regeneration of the West is unlikely to come about of its own accord. It will require a structure and a motivating force. Let me finally, therefore, consider a possible framework for such an arrangement, together with an outline of its terms of reference.

CHAPTER NINE

PEACE FROM STRENGTH

F REE TRADE IS a necessary but not a sufficient condition for world peace. Global peace will be assured only so long as there is a mechanism for containing the forces of expansionism wherever they may emerge. I have suggested that China in particular may develop pretensions to extend her borders.

In these circumstances, the West must stand ready to defend her values. In this way, as during the Cold War with the Soviet Union, she may never have the need to fight. The maintenance of free trade should at least assure the existence of a rational regime in China, one that will take heed of a clear determination in the West if necessary to make a military stand. As with the Cold War, the very act of defiance, if credible, will be the best deterrent against war. In this context, the NATO structure is the best available upon which to build a mechanism for coordinating not only Western defense but the values that should hold it together.

The North Atlantic Treaty signed in Washington on 4 April 1949 was indeed a statement of faith in Western values as much as it was the basis of a military alliance:

Spanish foreign policy has been distorted for some time from its natural patterns. Following decades of isolation under Franco, and with conservative ideas discredited, Spain put its trust wholly in the Socialist government of Felipe Gonzalez. In the aftermath of Franco's demise, Europe was seen to represent progress and the modern world. It was a way to anchor democracy in Spain; it stood for all the cultural freedoms Spain had been denied, the social revolutions that had passed it by. Added to this emotional appeal was the hard and tangible advantage of structural funds.

Gonzalez threw himself wholeheartedly into Europe. In his own terms, he was successful. Throughout the 1980s and early 1990s, Spain frequently won settlements from the EU that its size and importance did not appear to merit, from increases in the cohesion and structural funds to vast new fish quotas. A cynic might characterize Gonzalez's strategy as one of agreeing to every federalist measure proposed by France and Germany in return for substantial handouts. In those terms, it worked.

The result of Spain's obsession with European integration has been that it has neglected its wider ties and responsibilities. This, however, has been an aberration. The government's European policy has not altered people's sense of cultural or blood relation. As center-right ideas become rehabilitated and the Socialist star wanes, Spain is reassessing its place in the world.

Europe is no longer viewed as a symbol of freedom and progress. Many Spaniards resent what they perceive as an excessive dependence on France, a country they view in much the same way that Frenchmen view Germany. They feel that Gonzalez's special relationship with President Mitterrand often led to the eclipse of Spanish interests by European interests. Many Spaniards who value the unity of Spain dislike the way the EU encourages regionalism. Even the cohesion funds are no longer thought of as an unmixed blessing. Several Spanish economists have begun to point out that the price demanded for this assistance is that Spain give up her natural advantages of low costs and competitive devaluation so as to meet EU convergence criteria. The Maastricht process has led to massive unemployment, especially in the textile and agricultural sectors, as companies relocate to North Africa, and the government is prevented from using monetary policy to tackle the employment problem. Cohesion handouts, it is argued, are not adequate compensation for this damage, since they do not go to the workers who have suffered but to a handful of corrupt officials. Spain does not want to become a pensioner, reliant on subsidies from Germany and Britain as compensation for the business it has lost by complying with Maastricht.

This kind of thinking is found especially on the Spanish right, which, twenty years after Franco, has shed the stigma once attached to it. It goes hand-in-hand with a sense that Spain must rediscover its Atlantic identity.

A good example of Spain's new Atlanticism can be found in the policies of the Partido Popular. Its leader and new Prime Minister, José Maria Aznar, has recently written thus on the need for Spain to rediscover its "transatlantic destiny:"

> Spain is not just a Mediterranean country. Its Atlantic face, gazing out to America, was not given enough attention when our foreign policy was being drawn up during recent years. We must recover it, for it would be a historical suicide to renounce or disregard Spain's Atlantic identity.
>
> The Ibero-American community of nations is inseparable from Spain. Any policy which fails to take account of this fact will be dashed against a historical reality which, properly assumed, will yield enormous benefits to all. Over several

visits I have seen proof that this reality is tangible, that it is alive, although the policies which have prevailed recently have failed to take account of it.

We have to speak in a new language: the language of the creative, efficient and productive market where technological research and progress take pride of place. Spanish businessmen, technicians, professionals and academics must discover and take advantage of the great opportunities offered today by America. Spain is interested in an open Europe, far from the spectre of a "fortress Europe" which occasionally haunts our continent. Our ties to Latin America are a good reason for this. I think that, because of the importance of their relations with Europe, because of the spectacular growth of their markets and because of the development of democracy on the continent, the Latin American countries deserve priority position in the Community's foreign policy, and it is appropriate for Spain to be their chief protector.

These feelings are also stirring in Portugal. There, too, the center-right has finally shaken off the impediment of its association with dictatorship. Very few Portuguese politicians today were old enough to be active under Salazar. Like their Spanish colleagues, Portuguese conservatives watched impotently for two decades as successive Socialist governments tamely acquiesced in the European federal process in return for Cohesion handouts. Portugal's links with its former colonies have been weakened, many of its natural competitive advantages have been lost, and its economy has become increasingly reliant on EU payments.

As in Spain, there is now a discernible backlash from the right. Portugal's main right-wing party, the Partido Popular, has fiercely opposed the Maastricht process and especially plans for monetary union. Portuguese conservatives see a wholesale restructuring of the economy, with massive deregulation and privatization, as an alternative to European social and monetary convergence. They regard European harmonization policies as an attempt by the wealthier countries to export their high costs and uncompetitive practices. They are keen to build up a Lusophone (Portuguese speaking) community once again as an antidote to excessive reliance on Europe. And they share the determination of the nonsocialist parties in Britain and Spain that the EU should never become introverted or protectionist.

These policies are not distant aspirations. They are regarded as being of the utmost immediate concern. The Partido Popular's manifesto is centered on the proposal to repeal Maastricht, rule out monetary union, and extend links with the Portuguese-speaking nations overseas. When Iberia eventually throws off Socialism, which has held sway since the demise of the dictatorships, its attitude to Europe and the world will alter sharply. The weltanschauung one would expect from seafaring Atlantic states will reemerge.

That there should be any danger of the West dividing against itself is a telling comment on our age. The anti-Atlanticist tendency in the EU has for a long time held up the United States as a cultural enemy against which Europe must unite. When this tendency translates into economic policy, as it began to do during the completion of the Uruguay round of GATT, there is serious cause for concern. When it begins to provoke a reaction from the Western hemisphere, time is truly running out.

The political and economic reforms undertaken by the states of Latin America have placed those nations firmly back in the mainstream of Western development. The religious, philosophical, cultural, and political traditions of the Latin countries are not separate from those of Europe or the United States; they are part of a common Western heritage.

There is thus a very strong case for dropping the N from NATO and turning it into the basis for the widest possible alliance of democratic states—bonded together by cultural, political, and economic forces.

Nor is there any reason why it should be restricted to continents linked by the Atlantic. Ultimately, and sensibly, it would include all countries embracing a liberal, capitalistic democracy. It may come to be called the Western Treaty Organization.

The issue, of course, is this: would such an organization be unnecessarily provocative and divisive? Far from helping to safeguard world peace and security, would it itself become a cause of instability?

The answer lies partly in whether or not you think that the world today is irreversibly divided by contrasting and deep-rooted differences of approach to the governance of nations. I do. I have argued that the Confucian and the Christian traditions are very different, so different, indeed, as in most respects to be antithetical. The only issue is whether or not these differences are so great as to lead to ever-increasing mistrust, ultimately perhaps to war. The view that I have expressed in this book is that the differences can be contained through a mixture of free trade and a firmness in the West about minimum human and democratic rights, together with an acceptance that these will be applied differently in the East and the West.

This is in no way to deny to world bodies such as the United Nations and the World Trade Organization (WTO) an important and hopefully increasing role in the spreading of liberal values and thus in bringing nations into greater harmony with each other. This is particularly true of the World Trade Organization, with its newly acquired role of breaking down all barriers to free trade. It is certainly the case that the United States and the European Union were misguided in blocking China's application, on 19 December 1994, for membership of the WTO. Even if it were true that China were an exceptionally restrictive force in world trade—and the evidence is against this—membership of the WTO ought to encourage it to be less so.

The problem is that, however specific and enlightened their charters, the great international bodies—even the WTO—are bound to be as much concerned with searching for a consensus (at the lowest common denominator) as they are to proselytize a particular point of view. That is why, in the foreseeable future, effective pressure to match freer trade with the values associated with human rights and democracy will be maintained only if the nations of Europe and the Americas unite behind it.

There needs to be a formal coming together of the nations that subscribe to the beliefs of Western liberalism. This will require the services of a permanent institution. The pact will first and foremost involve a reaffirmation of beliefs but, like NATO, it will also have a defense commitment. Whether this organization is called the Western Treaty Organization does not matter. What does matter is that the West should not only reforge its beliefs, but should be prepared in the last resort to defend them.

Such a pact will best be made if it is organized on a nation-to-nation basis. An alliance of trade blocs—for instance, between the EU and NAFTA—founded as each is on a spurious unity and on the concept of trade preference rather than trade freedom, on the building of external barriers with third countries rather than on their removal, would not do. The nation-state remains the true unit of democracy; there is allegiance and there is accountability within the boundaries of the nation. The coming together

2. Only signatories of the European Convention on Human Rights should qualify for membership of the European Union.

3. Any state meeting the above qualification should be eligible for membership of the European Union subject only to the approval of the European Council.

II. THE WIDER EUROPE

Eastward enlargement must be a top priority for the EU. The current EU policies of excluding cheap imports and dumping subsidised products abroad are paid for ultimately by the EU citizen, who is penalised as a consumer and a taxpayer respectively. These policies, moreover, create population pressures on the Union's borders, damage the standing of Europe in the world and boost anti-Western forces in Eastern Europe, thereby threatening the stability of the entire continent. In order to accommodate the states of Central and Eastern Europe, the EU must be prepared to undergo significant structural changes.

4. The EU must work towards the admission of the Central and Eastern European nations as early as possible.

5. A timetable for membership should be drawn up, aimed at integrating the four Visegrad countries by 1 January 2000. Firm calendars should also be drawn up for the membership of other democratic states wishing to join.

6. The EU must drop its insistence on the acceptance in full of the *acquis communautaire* and the *finalité politique* by all new members.

7. Non-EU states should be able to integrate some specific policies—transport, energy or environmental protection, for

example—into EU structures while retaining control over other areas. This process will be facilitated by the unbundling of the EU's policy areas into different communities with different memberships as referred to below.

8. There must be a clear division of responsibilities among the different international organisations in Europe. The EU's ambition to arrogate to itself the functions which lie within the authority of other bodies must be circumscribed. The current and clearly understood division of responsibilities should be preserved and reaffirmed: human rights abuses should be the province of the Council of Europe, national minorities should be dealt with by the OSCE, defence should be the business of NATO and the WEU and so on.

III. CONSENT AND FLEXIBILITY

In a Union which is both expanding physically and extending its jurisdiction, it will be impossible to continue to demand unanimity and common action from all Member States in all areas. The development of a Multi-Track Europe, a Europe of many parts, builds on the growing precedent that not all twelve countries need participate in each new extension of EU authority: the Schengen Group, for example, operates within EU structures without covering all members; Greece never participated in the EMS; Britain has opted out of EU social policy and, along with Denmark, may opt out of EMU.

The Union cannot flourish if its Member States are forced against their will to participate in policies which are not in their interests. The principle of flexible integration among different groups of countries within the framework of a lightly but effec-

arbiter of the Treaties and, like all similar institutions, it has displayed an inherent tendency to agglomerate power. Action is therefore also needed at Member State level to prevent the continuous growth of power at the centre.

18. The formula which guarantees national sovereignty in areas of purely domestic concern should not only be written into the Treaties; it should also be included according to national circumstances in the constitutions of the Member States and enshrined by Act of Parliament in the United Kingdom.

19. A list should be drawn up to clarify the areas covered. It should include the voting system, local and regional government, foreign affairs, defence, immigration, education, health, industrial relations, social welfare and taxation. This list should also be incorporated as far as possible in the constitutions of the Member States.

20. The supremacy of national parliaments and governments will be guaranteed in these areas. Any EU directive or regulation covering them will be treated as advisory.

VI. INSTITUTIONAL REFORM

The Commission

21. The Commission should acknowledge that its role is that of an EU civil service carrying out the will of elected ministers.

22. Lacking a democratic mandate, it must lose the right to initiate legislation.

23. The practice of appointing senior politicians to the Commission should be ended: the Commission should be in the hands of able civil servants.

24. The number of Commissioners should be fixed, so as to prevent a constant increase in the number of portfolios created.

25. Commission officials must be made explicitly subject to cross-examination by the committees of national parliaments.

The European Parliament

26. National parliaments and governments should be acknowledged as the basic unit of democracy in Europe. The democratic deficit cannot be filled without strengthening the role of national parliaments within the EU decision-making process.

27. The European Parliament must explicitly be prohibited from interfering in those areas of policy which are reserved for national governments.

28. The European Parliament should focus on its original role of scrutinising the work of the Commission.

The European Court of Justice

29. The European Court must be denied the policy-making legislative function which it has been adopting in practice, as exemplified by cases such as *Costa*, *Van Duyn* and *Defrenne v Sabena*.

30. The direct applicability of European law should be strictly confined to areas necessary for the maintenance of a free internal market.

31. Court proceedings should be published so that the number of judges dissenting from a judgement and their reasons for disagreeing may be seen.

should be seen as a matter of essentially national concern (such as agriculture once the CAP has been repatriated).

39. The Union must abandon its import duties on Eastern and Central European produce, including agriculture, coal, steel and textiles.

40. Conscious of the implications of Eastward enlargement, of the need to avoid traumatic social disruption and of the specificity of national conditions in agriculture, the EU should move to return responsibility for agricultural policy and farm subsidies to the Member States.

41. Subsidies at EU level should be phased out. Democratic accountability suffers when taxpayers in one country are subsidising industries in another.

IX. THE BUDGET

The EU budget is made up from three forms of revenue: agricultural levies and customs duties (around 23 percent); VAT contributions (approximately 55 percent) and a GDP-based payment (22 percent). 82 percent of the budget goes on agriculture and structural operations, while the rest goes on administration, research projects, overseas aid, etc.

42. Eventual repatriation of the CAP (including all parts of the European Agricultural Guidance and Guarantee Fund) would reduce the overall budget by around 65 percent.

43. The gradual reduction of the Cohesion Fund and of agricultural spending should be accompanied by more effective

direction of the Structural Funds to minimise bureaucracy and waste.

44. The remaining budget should be met entirely by a GDP-based contribution from the Member States. EU "own resources," which give the Union a vested interest in a protectionist trade policy, should be abolished.

X. A DEFENCE IDENTITY

The current position under Maastricht provides for the WEU to be built up as the defence arm of the Union while at the same time "respecting the obligations of certain Member States under the North Atlantic Treaty." The defence provisions of the Treaty are largely intergovernmental, although "the Commission shall be fully associated with the work carried out in the common foreign and security policy field." Pressure is building to bring defence fully under Commission jurisdiction in 1996.

45. The aim of replacing multilateral action with unanimous foreign policy should be recognised as inherently undesirable: it will tend to produce the policy of the lowest common denominator, the position which least offends. In Bosnia, the only policy capable of attracting unanimous support was one of doing essentially nothing.

46. The WEU plays a useful role as the European pillar of the Atlantic Alliance, but it can never replace NATO. Only NATO with a US presence is capable of producing key strategic components such as reconnaissance satellites, air- and sea-lift fleets, advanced military computers and missile defence.

47. The EU as a whole should not in itself require a defence

Community law), thereby giving legal recognition to this process for the first time.

A further problem lies in the motivation of the central institutions of the EU. Both the Commission and the European Court of Justice see their role as being to bring as many fields of policy as possible into the EU's administrative domain. As long ago as 1970, the Commission was defined as "at one and the same time the guardian of the Treaties and the motive force for integration."[1] The Commission is not only given the authority to hasten moves to integration between and outside the Treaties, but in fact defines its success in terms of doing so. A former Secretary-General of the Commission, writing in an official EC publication in 1988, explained its powers clearly. *"Everything to do with economic union was left blank in the Treaty, but blanks can be filled by the institutions. There is no need for fresh treaties or fresh parliamentary ratification."*[2]

The European Court takes the same line, but with even more serious consequences. Like the Commission, it defines its success in terms of promoting integration, in the *Netherlands v. High Authority* case of 1960, the power of the Court to rule on complaints against Member States was described as "the *ultima ratio* enabling the Community interests enshrined in the Treaty to prevail over the inertia and resistance of the Member States." The Court's judgements are final and binding; there is no appeal beyond them. Its methods are therefore crucially important. There is now an almost complete consensus among lawyers across Europe that the European Court has ceased simply to perform an interpretative or judicial function and has adopted a policy-making or

---

[1] Franco Malfatti, President of the European Commission, 1970.
[2] Emile Noël, Office for Official Publications of the European Communities, L-2985 Luxembourg.

legislative role.[3] There are several cases where the Court's judgements have undeniably ignored the law as written in favour of the law as the European Court would like it to be written. The cases of *Costa v. ENEL (1964)*, *Van Duyn v. Home Office (1974)* and *Defrenne v. Sabena (1976)* are among the many clear examples of the European Court going well beyond the written text to make policy on its own.[4]

A final cause for concern is the supremacy of EU law over the legal systems of the Member States. The Treaty of Rome differs from other international treaties in that it requires its provisions, as well as the regulations of the institutions established under it, to be incorporated as part of the internal laws of its Member States. EU legislation is thus directly binding on people and businesses within the Member States. National courts are required to give precedence to EU law over national law—even if the national legislation is adopted subsequently to the EU legislation. Since the UK's accession to the Community in 1972, all Acts of Parliament which are deemed inadvertently to contradict Community law have been modified so as to comply with the European Communities Act. The question of whether an Act of Parliament might deliberately override Community law was for a long time a matter for debate. In the *Factortame* case of 1991, however, the European Court ruled that British courts had been right to suspend the 1988 Merchant Shipping Act which had sought to end the practice whereby Spanish fishermen registered themselves as Brit-

---

[3] Among the best works on this subject in English are: H. Schermera, *The European Court of Justice: Promoter of Integration*, 1974; Gavin Smith, *The European Court of Justice: Judges or Policy Makers?* 1990; and Martin Howe, *European and the Constitution After Maastricht*, 1992.

[4] See especially Sir Patrick Neill QC, *The European Court of Justice: A Case Study in Judicial Activism*, 1995.

No other EU country has displayed the United Kingdom's reluctance to assert itself in European negotiations. Over the last three years, Italy has been officially awarded an extra milk quota which it effectively stole; Spain has won an increase in the Cohesion Fund and access to British fishing grounds; Germany has secured the Central Bank; France has won a new European Parliament building, protection for its film industry and more money for its farmers after the GATT agreement. None of these achievements can be dressed up as matters of principle, yet all were won through sheer determination. Britain, which is financially critical to the other members and which can argue a case that is not only principled but popular across Europe is in a far stronger position than its timidity to date might suggest.

VARIABLE GEOMETRY

Britain's negotiating strength notwithstanding, it must be conceded that the majority of European governments will not easily be diverted from their declared ambition to forge ahead with full political and economic integration. Their leaders have invested considerable political capital in securing a further move towards European unity in 1996. In particular, they want a common foreign and defence policy, more powers for the European Parliament, an erosion of the national veto and EU control over the intergovernmental pillars of Maastricht. Yet their very determination can be turned to Britain's advantage.

Any move towards further integration within EU structures will require a change to the Treaties. Under Article 236 of the Treaty of Rome, all alterations to the Treaties must be unanimous. Britain thus has an unequivocal right of veto.

It is quite true that a group of Member States could pursue further integration on their own in some separate organisation outside the treaties. Britain could do nothing to prevent them: it could not have vetoed the establishment of the Schengen Group, for example, any more than Ireland or Denmark can arrest the development of the WEU. The reality, however, is that the other Member States are not interested in pursuing political or economic union except within the main body of the EU. The Maastricht negotiations demonstrate this point well. It would have been perfectly possible for the continental governments to adopt the Social Charter in a subcommunity outside the Treaties. It would likewise have been possible to move to economic and monetary union through a separate structure. In both cases, the other Member States were determined to move ahead within the existing Treaties, granting Britain (and later Denmark) opt-outs. Their attitude is quite understandable. There would be a heavy political and economic cost in setting up a parallel structure to administer an "inner core," with its own Commission, its own Parliament etc. The populations of the "inner core" states would be unhappy at the prospect of inclusion in a tight and regulated union, the Mediterranean countries would fiercely resent being left out and the potential for confusion or conflict between the two structures would be considerable. European political leaders have absolutely no appetite for integration outside the corpus of the EU.

This gives Britain its strongest negotiating counter of all. The other states need Britain's permission to forge ahead on their own. Since failure to secure further integration is unthinkable to a number of their governments and since they will not pursue such integration except within the Treaties, Britain can effectively name its own price for withholding its veto. If the government is serious about remaining outside a federal state, that price must be a net retrieval of power. One way to ensure that the United Kingdom is not drawn into a political union is to amend the 1972 European Communities Act so that the ultimate supremacy of the British Parliament is guaranteed in certain fields of purely domestic concern (health, education, the voting system, local government, industrial relations, defence, law and taxation). This would represent a major recovery of self-government by the United Kingdom and would protect it from future moves to centralisation. It would of course require a change to the Treaty. While the other Member States would not be happy at this prospect, they would almost certainly accept it as the price for pursuing their own ambitions within the EU. Many of them have in any case come to resent being held back by a single country which always forces the entire Union to slow to its own pace. Put bluntly, if the price for taking several steps forward is allowing Britain to take a few paces back, most continental governments would be prepared to pay.

To succeed with so ambitious a strategy will not necessarily be easy, but the potential gains are considerable. A looser and more practical association with the EU, based on mutual interests, would remove the resentment which has poisoned Britain's European policy until now. Moreover, if Britain were to put its membership of the EU on a new basis, pressure would grow for the other Member States similarly to adjust their relationships with Brussels. This would mean a major step towards the kind of European Union to which successive British governments have always aspired. If Britain fails to emerge from 1996 having recouped significant powers, nothing will prevent its eventual drift into a federal Europe.

*List of those who attended the European Research Group
Conferences of Parliamentarians held at Brasenose College,
Oxford, on 16 and 17 September 1994 and at the National
Assembly, Paris, on 9 and 10 December 1994 and in
Brussels on 23 June 1995.*

AKARCALI, Bülent, MP	Motherland Party	Turkey
BARBIER, Bernard, Senator	UDF	France
BELIEN, Paul	Centre for the New Europe	Belgium
BOLKESTEIN, Frits, MP	VVD	Netherlands
BONSOR, Sir Nicholas, Bt, MP	Conservative Party	United Kingdom
DEL CASTILLO, Professor Pilar	Popular Party	Spain
CATALA, Nicole, MP	RPR	France
CORREIA DE SÁ, Dr Salvador	CDS-Popular Party	Portugal
CORTÉS MARTÍN, Miguel, MP	Popular Party	Spain
COUGHLAN, Anthony	National Platform	Ireland
CRAN, James, MP	Conservative Party	United Kingdom
DI MUCCIO, On. Pietro, MP	Forza Italia	Italy
DOMINATI, Laurent, MP	UDF	France
FREY, Claude, MP	Radical Democratic Party	Switzerland

GENNSER, Margit, MP	Moderate Party	Sweden
GRIOTTERAY, Alain, MP	UDF	France
GUNDERSEN, Frank Fridtjof, MP	Progress Party	Norway
HAGEN, Carl I, MP	Progress Party	Norway
HALL, Aleksander, MP	Conservative Party	Poland
HØGLUND, Morten	Progress Party	Norway
LAWRENCE, Sir Ivan, QC, MP	Conservative Party	United Kingdom
LOMBARD, Maurice, Senator	RPR	France
LUMMER, Heinrich, MP	CDU	Germany
MACEK, Miroslav	ODS	Czech Republic
MIKOLÁSIK, Miroslav, MP	KDH	Slovakia
MURER, Gerulf, MP	FPÖ	Austria
MYARD, Jacques, MP	RPR	France
NÉMETH, Zsolt, MP	Fidesz	Hungary
NOBRE GUEDES, Dr Luís	CDS-Popular Party	Portugal
PANDRAUD, Robert, MP	RPR	France
PEARSON of RANNOCH, Lord	Conservative Party	United Kingdom
RAMSAUER, Dr Peter, MP	CSU	Germany
REICHOLD, Ing. Mathias, MP	FPÖ	Austria
RIESS, Susanne, Senator	FPÖ	Austria
ROSSO, On. Robert, MP	Forza Italia	Italy
SANDOZ, Suzette, MP	Liberal Party	Switzerland
SAVARESE, On. Dott. Enzo, MP	Forza Italia	Italy
SIMÕES DIAS, Dr João Pedro	CDS-Popular Party	Portugal
SKAARUP, Peter	Progress Party	Denmark
SNÆHÓLM, Jón Kristinn	Independence Party	Iceland
SPICER, Michael, MP (Chairman)	Conservative Party	United Kingdom
TAYLOR, Rt Hon John, MP	Ulster Unionist Party	United Kingdom
TIMERMANS DEL OLMO, Alfredo	Popular Party	Spain
THULESEN DAHL, Kristian, MP	Progress Party	Denmark
UIDAL QUADRAS, Aleix	Popular Party	Spain
VAN DER WAAL, Leen, MP	SGP	Netherlands
WETTERSTAD, Roy N, MP	Free Democrats	Norway